Wendy Underhill is retired and lives in north Wiltshire, close to her family. Primarily she was a mother and housewife until, when in her fifties, after training, spent time in Southern Africa as a missionary and finally went to Namibia to help set up an HIV/Aids project for a church.

When she is not looking after her grand-children, she enjoys being a part of her local church, community and volunteering with the National Trust.

JUST TO BE LOVED

A Journey to Find Forgiveness and Acceptance

Wendy Underhill

JUST TO BE LOVED

A Journey to Find Forgiveness and Acceptance

When Jesus says, 'Come and see,' there is no knowing where the journey may lead. Only when we follow will we discover for ourselves the answer to his question: 'What are you looking for?' Perhaps the answer is: 'You!'[1]

Vanguard Press

---

[1] Margaret Silf, *New Daylight* (The Bible Reading Fellowship 2009), p.41.

A CIP catalogue record for this title is
available from the British Library.

ISBN 978 1 84386 844 6

*Vanguard Press is an imprint of
Pegasus Elliot MacKenzie Publishers Ltd.*
www.pegasuspublishers.com

First Published in 2012

**Vanguard Press
Sheraton House Castle Park
Cambridge England**

Printed & Bound in Great Britain

Disclaimer

Some names have been changed to protect identities.

Every effort to contact holders of copyright has been made; to those yet to have provided formal permission please do contact the publisher.

Acknowledgements

To my three wonderful and beautiful daughters, Louise, Mary and Jane. Thank you for your love and support in letting me go to help those in need. Also to my grand-daughters, Rose and Grace, who give me such joy and laughter in my senior years; thank you girls!

To all my family and friends who have played such an important part in my life over the years. Thank you for believing that I have a story that needs to be told. You know who you are!

To Esme Nourse. Thank you for all of your help in editing and also your continual encouragement which was so often needed.

To all the staff at Pegasus who were involved, and especially Mercy Kaggwa for her patience in answering my endless questions.

For Mum who never forgot me.

Contents

Part Two: A True Identity

PREFACE

You were in God's mind before you were in your mother's womb. Your parents didn't create you – God did. It doesn't matter if you were conceived during an act of date rape, or born to a mother on income support who had children by several different fathers, God created you! He didn't allow you to be aborted, miscarried, stillborn or die in childhood. Those events didn't take you. Why? Because God isn't finished with you yet. Don't forget that!

Even when you were abused as a child, He never took His hand off you. He brought you through and kept you from losing your mind. He's the One who brought you to an understanding of Jesus Christ as your Lord and Saviour. He's the One who raised you up in spite of every attempt of the enemy to destroy you, diminish you, defame you, or discourage you.

The fact is, if you hadn't gone through everything you've been through, you wouldn't be the person you are today – and God knows that! He has been in the process of creating you, moulding you, refining and perfecting you since the moment He first thought of you. He gave you your own personality, your own abilities, your own spiritual gifts and your own identity in Christ. Why? So that you, and you alone, might praise Him the way you do, give the way you do, serve the way you do, and love the way you do. Rejoice: you're His unique creation and He loves you!

I knew you before time began. I even know how many hairs are on your head! Like parent, like child; you're created in My image. Not only have I got plans for you, I've also given you the talents needed to fulfil them. And what I give, nobody else can take away. But don't neglect them; remember to exercise them and stir them up daily.

Rest assured that I've started a good work in you and I'm going to finish it. I always complete what I begin. My Word concerning you is forever settled in heaven. My commitment to you is unending. In this life, you'll have challenges, but cheer up; I've robbed Satan of his power to hurt you, and the world of its power to destroy you! When you're in trouble, remember I'm a very present help. Give Me your burdens and I'll sustain you. When you're stressed-out or weighed down by the pressures of life, lean on Me, I'll be your Rock, your Fortress, your Deliverer and your Strength. Even though you fall from time to time, you won't be destroyed, because I'm holding you.

But a word of caution: don't take advice from those who are spiritually blind, and don't hang out with sceptics. Delight yourself in My Word, and like a big oak tree growing by a river you'll be fruitful and prosper in all that you do.

Do you know there are people who are literally 'off limits' to Satan? It's not that they're spiritual giants; it's that they're vital to God's plans. They're ordinary clay pots filled with extraordinary ointment. The glory doesn't come from them – but from what God's placed inside them. As a result, Satan can't touch them. God specialises in restoring broken vessels. He takes things that aren't productive… marriages that don't work… people who've failed… and teaches them how to be victorious and fruitful in His service.

Knowing this can give you the tenacity and strength to face whatever comes. Because you know that when God places His treasure inside you, unless He takes you down, nothing else can![2]

---

[2] Based on Ephesians 1: 4. Source and author unknown.

PART ONE
A LOST IDENTITY

CHAPTER 1

The Fortune Teller's Predictions

But the plans of the Lord stand firm forever.

(Psalm 33:11)

I had never been to a fortune teller before. Aunty Mary loved all that sort of thing. She had a set of tarot cards that she would occasionally take out to read and one day she told me I would marry a tall fair-haired man. Aunty Mary was an old friend of my mother's and she had invited me to go with her to visit her cousins in Cheshire for a holiday. I had just sat my 'O' levels and with all my friends away on their summer holidays it was a good opportunity to do something different. Every summer in the village where her cousins lived they had a fair and a fortune teller was always there.

I was nervous waiting in the queue. Did I really want to know what the future held for me? Would it turn out as I was told? Would my life begin to revolve around these predictions? But then I didn't have to believe what she told me. And she couldn't tell me anything worse than the dream I had had so long ago, which had come true. Lost in my thoughts I suddenly became aware that Aunty Mary was speaking to me, "It's your turn now. I'll wait for you just here."

I nodded my head and with great trepidation walked up the steps of the small caravan. It was dark inside after the bright sunlight and it took me a few moments to adjust my eyes.

"Come in," said a voice with a slight foreign accent. "Come and sit down here."

Just inside the door was a table with a crystal ball on a stand. The voice was coming from a dark-skinned lady sitting at the table wearing a colourful floral dress, with a cream shawl over her shoulders and a blue scarf around her head. She had large glass beads around her neck and long dangling ear rings. She motioned for me to sit down opposite her and held out her hand for the 2s 6d Aunty Mary had given me. She then asked me my name. "Wendy," I replied.

For what seemed like forever, I sat watching her as she placed her hands around the ball chanting to herself. I was just about ready to get up and leave as I thought nothing was going to happen, when she said,

"You're soon going to receive some news in a brown envelope." What a strange thing to predict. Some more silence. "You had a difficult and unhappy childhood and your Mother had to give you away and you went to live with strangers."

I was startled. How did she know that by just gazing into a ball? It was years now since I had thought about Mum and wanting to see her again. Somehow I had managed to adjust to a new life with a new identity. "Don't worry," she continued. "You will meet up with her again and it will be a joyous reunion." And then she went back to gazing into her ball leaving me wondering if it would indeed come true.

"You will get married, but it won't be a happy marriage and sometime during your marriage you will live in a large white house."

Once more she placed her hands around her ball, but it would seem she couldn't see anything else as she said, "That's all for now."

I stepped back into the bright sunshine.

"How did you get on?" asked Aunty Mary. "Did she tell you anything good?"

I didn't like to tell her about Mum as I we had never discussed it with her, so I just told her I was going to get married one day, live in a large white house and receive some news in a brown envelope in the post. She seemed satisfied with my answer and we went to join her cousins for a cup of tea for them and an ice cream for me.

It wasn't until I was lying in bed that night that I was able to think more about what the fortune teller had told me. News in a brown envelope was rather obvious as I knew my 'O' level results were coming in a 'brown' envelope. Getting married was great. Even at the age of sixteen I wasn't really interested in having a career and still had no idea what I wanted to do. Jobs were so easy to come by, so I didn't have to plan too far ahead. All I really wanted to do with my life was to meet the right person, get married and have a family of my own and living in a large white house sounded rather nice. I know she had said it wouldn't be a happy marriage, but then how did she know about Mum? Would I really see her again? I had no idea where she was and she wouldn't know where I was. The whole thing was totally impossible; therefore she was probably wrong about me having an unhappy marriage.

Somehow though I knew my life would now revolve around these predictions as I would never forget what she had told me.

As I drifted off to sleep I began to remember once more that terrible day when I last saw Mum.

CHAPTER 2

Adoption

As a mother comforts her child, so I will comfort you.
(Isaiah 66.13)

I was frightened and didn't want to leave Mum again. Yesterday some strange lady had tried to take me away from her and then we had gone to Great Uncle Kenneth's home in London for the night and now, after breakfast, Dad had told me I had to go with him. If I made any more fuss, then I knew what was coming to me. He was cross, but that wasn't unusual either.

So I kept quiet and said a quick 'goodbye' to Mum and meekly followed him, too scared of him to do anything other than hold onto his hand. It was a hot August day and I found it difficult at times to keep up with Dad's pace as we hurried to catch a bus and then the tube. Where were we going? Mum didn't usually leave me on my own with him.

We eventually arrived at a department store and went into the men's section where Dad started to look at some ties. I wandered around getting bored and found an aquarium with lots of small brightly coloured fish swimming amongst some weeds. I kept one eye on Dad as I wasn't used to being in such a big shop and could see he was getting agitated. Then he saw a lady coming into the shop and went across to talk to her. I had never seen this lady before, but Dad told me I was to go with her. Her name was Miss Gates. He didn't bother to say 'goodbye' and quickly left the shop. We then went in a taxi to Waterloo Station and boarded a train to a place called Winchester.

For most of the journey, when I wasn't eating some jam sandwiches which Miss Gates gave me, I looked out of the window at the passing scenery. What was happening to me? Where was Mum? Why wasn't she here with me? I didn't like to ask in case Dad suddenly appeared.

When we arrived in Winchester we took another taxi and got out at what seemed to be an enormous house, on a busy main road where Miss Gates knocked on the black door using the brass knocker in the shape of a lion's head. It was quickly opened by a man and a lady, who after greeting us, led us through another door into the garden, where I found a pram with a doll in it and some other toys to play with.

This new lady, who was called Mrs Oxley, and had dark curly hair similar to mine, gave us some sandwiches and cake to eat, but I wasn't very hungry. When she and the man, who was called Dr Oxley, asked me some questions about myself, I didn't know how to respond and just nodded my head. They then tried to explain to me that they were going to be my new Mummy and Daddy. But that didn't make sense because I already had a Mum and a Dad, and a younger sister and baby brother – I didn't need any more parents. Where were they? So I just kept quiet and went on playing with my new toys while they talked to the other lady.

I drifted off into my dream world where everything was just right – being with Mum, Tina and Chris, laughing and playing happily together and not living in any fear of Dad –

and not like the other dream I had recently had of walking alone along a cold, dark, deserted sandy beach which had ended in a hill. I had felt as if no one wanted or cared about me and it gave me an overwhelming sense of desolation. Was this dream coming true now?

I was brought back to reality with Daddy, as I was to call him, turning to me and asking,

"Would you like to go with me to the corner shop? I need to buy some cigarettes and perhaps you would like some sweets?"

With sweets still on ration and a novelty to me, as we only had them on special occasions, I quickly said 'yes'.

It was wonderful wandering around the small dark shop trying to decide what to have and in the end I chose some sherbet lemons as I knew they would last a long time. We hadn't been gone very long and on our return I discovered Miss Gates had gone.

The rest of the day passed in a haze. My new Mummy took me upstairs to my new bedroom where I found a pile of new clothes, which was also very strange as I had clothes back home and where was my teddy bear which always came to bed with me? The bedroom was enormous compared to the one back home, which I shared with Tina and Chris. I was shown the bathroom and quickly had a bath. Then both Mummy and Daddy tucked me up in bed, kissed me 'good night' and left me to sleep. But all I could do was bury my head under the blankets, put my thumb in my mouth and cry and cry.

Where was Mum? Why had she abandoned me? Will she come back and take me home tomorrow? Somehow I knew she wouldn't be coming back. Within a matter of a few hours everything that had been so precious to me had been taken away. I was only four years old.

I was born on the 13th January 1945 in my maternal grandparents' home in Lyme Regis. When I was five weeks old Dad, who was in the Royal Air Force, was posted to Calshott just outside Southampton and we moved into some digs out in the country down a very muddy lane. The house had a tin roof, no running water or electricity and a landlady who wouldn't stop talking. Dad couldn't stand her chatter so we only stayed a month and went back to stay with my grandparents.

After Dad was demobbed he had a variety of jobs so we moved around. My sister Tina was born in June 1946 and when she was about a year old Dad decided to buy a boat for us all to live on, which he sailed from Chichester to Littlehampton and then up the River Arun to Arundel. Mum hated the boat and found it all a nightmare as even sitting in a boat in harbour made her feel seasick.

Dad didn't think it was worth commuting to London everyday so he would leave us all for three or four days at a time. By this time Mum was pregnant with my brother Chris and as we could only go on shore at certain times because of the tide, life became very difficult for her.

Finally one day when she felt she was going to have a miscarriage, she rang her parents and they came to our rescue. Chris was born the following March and we all moved once again, this time into a semi-detached Victorian house on a main road in Alton.

It was at this time that I began to realise how much Dad hated me, but I had no idea why. The only difference I could see was that I had dark curly hair and both Tina and Chris had straight fair hair. So why should that make a difference? Memories of this time are still hazy, but I can see us having meals in the kitchen and the sticky flypapers hanging from the ceiling, covered in dead flies.

There was a small garden with a patio which had a step leading up onto the lawns where Tina and I could play with our dolls. Mum had a fit one day when she caught me pushing Chris in his pram down that step! But despite all those outward signs and activities of normal post-war life in Hampshire, I felt far from safe. In fact, we all lived in fear.

I was a strong-willed child and at times got bored playing in the garden so one day I decided to take Tina on an adventure by going out of the front door, running round the corner of the house and back through the side gate into the garden. As we peeped round the door, we carefully looked up and down the road to make sure no one could see us before we sprinted quickly round into the garden. It was wonderful to feel so carefree, and literally stretch our legs on our self-made race track.

The rest of the day passed by as normal – playing with our toys, egg and bread soldiers for tea and then straight upstairs for a bath before bedtime. I was still in the bath when Dad came home from work. He burst into the room, grabbed my arm and dragged me out of the bath and into their bedroom. His breath smelled of alcohol, as he had had his usual whiskey before coming upstairs. I knew something was wrong and was scared. As we went past Mum's dressing table he picked up her hairbrush and pushed me into the middle of the room. With

Mum's hairbrush bristles-side down he beat me on my bare bottom several times.

"Don't you ever lead your sister astray again," he said, and then went out of the room leaving me cold, wet and shocked. Somehow, someone had seen us run round the house and told him. Mum came rushing into the room with a towel and held me close, but the stinging, both on my skin and in my eyes from the held-back salty tears, stayed with me long into the night.

Events like that became so normal, that it was only the extreme ones that now stick in my memory – like the occasion of Chris's birthday. We had been opening his presents in Mum and Dad's bedroom and somehow I lost the key to wind up the clock-work train he had been given. I was beaten for that too. With Dad's hatred of me becoming worse Mum began to get me ready for bed early and then leave me in an empty room in the attic until Dad had said good-night to Tina and Chris, and then she would come and fetch me and put me to bed.

I can also clearly recall walking down the road one day with Mum to the Doctor's surgery to collect a prescription for Dad and saying to Mum that I was glad he was ill and I hoped he would die. Was this the way I coped with the knowledge of his total hatred of me by wishing he would die? I do not know. Young as I was, I knew the way he treated me was not right.

I can remember too that it wasn't long after I was adopted that a strange thing happened. Daddy had decided he wanted to buy another car and had seen one he liked advertised in London. So on his day off Mummy and I went with him to view the car and on the way there we drove through Alton, Hampshire, and then passed the house where I had lived with Mum. I could not believe it – was Mum still there? I had shrunk back in my seat and not said anything. I was already developing a sense of responsibility, a change of identity, to try to be the person the people I was with wanted me to be. I knew I had to try to forget my old life, and Mum, Tina and Chris. I was now the daughter of Philip and Pat Oxley.

CHAPTER 3

Learning To Adjust

And God will wipe away every tear from their eyes.

(Rev.7:17)

How was I going to cope without Mum? Would I ever see her again? As well as trying to blot out what had happened to me, I also needed to build a wall around me so no one could get too close to me again and hurt me. I was going to be strong for myself and take control of my life.

I still cried myself to sleep most nights wondering where Mum, Tina and Chris were, but there was also a great relief that I no longer lived in fear of being beaten by Dad if I did something wrong. Instinctively I knew neither Daddy nor Mummy would ever hurt me either physically or mentally. But why had this happened to me? Why had I been abandoned? What had I done wrong? Was I so un-loveable? Would Mum remember me on my birthday and at Christmas? Or would she in time forget I existed? One day I would find her and get answers to my questions.

It took me several months, but gradually I became more used to my surroundings and to start to accept that I now had new parents to take care of me. Daddy was a GP running a single-handed practice and was a gentleman in the true sense of the word. He was kind, thoughtful, selfless, and generous. He had a quiet sense of humour, seeing the funny side of life and rarely lost his temper. He was devoted to Mummy and as a doctor, always put his patients first. I always felt closer to him than Mummy, possibly because I could 'wind him round my little finger' and get what I wanted!

Mummy had been a nurse so she helped him in his work. I know she loved me in her own way, but she didn't know how to show it and I desperately needed to be hugged and told I was loved, as Mum had done. So I was often cross with her and always felt I was low down in her list of priorities – she loved Daddy first, then helping him in the practice next and finally I felt I came third. It seemed that the only times I really felt her love was when I was ill.

I often suffered with earache and had several mastoids which were always operated on in my own bed. I dreaded the consultant Daddy would call in for confirmation. After examining me he would go back downstairs saying "I'll call the anaesthetist and let you know when I will operate. Should be all right for tomorrow".

I just could not stand the smell of the rubber of the gas mask, everything else I could cope with. So Mummy would smother the mask with her lavender water, and I would drift off to sleep smelling lavender and she would then take care of me as I recovered.

Living with us was Lily, Mummy's maid. She was a small, wiry lady with long grey hair which she rolled up into a bun. She cleaned the house and in the afternoons wore a black dress with a small white apron pinned to it. She answered the door, waited at table if my parents had guests and called

Mummy "Moom'. One morning Lily opened the door to a tall, well-built woman in her early forties, wearing a wonderful tall hat, like a flower pot, with a feather sticking out of it. Mrs Williams or 'Mrs Willums' as I would call her, came to help in the house as well. So along with Lily and Mrs Williams I didn't feel so lonely and when they had time they would often play with me.

Soon after Mrs Williams arrived I had measles and was confined to bed with the curtains drawn. Mummy would keep popping in to see if I was all right, but being a Monday morning she was busy helping Lily with the weekly wash, so when I was sick all over the bed clothes it was ages before she came back again to sort me out. Mrs Williams felt sorry for me and bought me a goldfish which I called 'Jim' after her husband and watching Jim swim round his bowl made me feel less lonely.

I wasn't without friends of my own age, though. I had not been living long with my new parents when I met Marg. I was skipping at the entrance to the drive at the side of the house and Marg who lived nearly opposite saw me and ran inside to fetch her rope. We then crept along the road until we were nearly opposite each other and began to copy each other with our skipping.

"Would you like to come for tea?" Marg asked after a while.

"Yes, please," I replied.

"I'll just go and ask Mummy if this is all right."

She came back a few minutes later and so began a life-long friendship with both her and her older sister Liz. Their garden backed onto a quiet side road and often Marg, Liz and I would go out there to play skipping games and we would soon attract other children to join in with us to play street games like 'Boatman, Boatman will you ferry me across the river?' or 'English Bulldog'. One day a policewoman came and told us to go home – we were soon back again when she had gone! It was good to have friends to play with and somewhere to play and it all helped me to adjust to being without my siblings.

During the summer Marg, Liz and I were allowed to buy ice-lollies from the corner shop and our respective mothers would take it in turns to pay for them. We were never allowed to eat them in the street, but would have the odd lick and put it back in its wrapper until we reached home – by which time it had nearly all gone! I was never allowed to play with Marg and Liz on a Sunday, as it was very much a family day.

I then made a third friend, Brenda, when we both had chicken-pox. Daddy was their doctor and on visiting Brenda had suggested that he bring me over, so we could keep each other company. So our friendship began with us sharing a bed, both covered in spots!

Soon after my fifth birthday I started at the preparatory school of St. Swithun's, a private school in Winchester, where I made some new friends and enjoyed the routine of school life. I was a slow learner and remained near the bottom of the class for most of my schooling, but no one seemed too concerned. Daddy would take me there in the mornings before surgery and Mummy would collect me at the end of the day when we would walk home and do some shopping on the way. I loved going into the side door of the chemist to their dispensary to collect my free orange juice and cod liver oil and any prescriptions Daddy needed for his patients. Daddy had his own dispensary and after morning made up various medicines for his patients to collect later on in the day. There were two medicines he regularly made up. One I loved the name of,

'Miss Pot Sit' (potassium citrate mixture for urinary infections), and another was a wonderful 'cough and spit' mixture when people had a bad cold. It tasted revolting but worked quickly to relieve congestion.

I became good friends with Jean and I can remember one holiday, when I was about six, she invited me to spend the day with her. Mummy knew Jean had had a two-wheeled bike for her birthday which was the day before mine.

"Under no circumstances are you to ride Jean's bike," she said as I went to get into her Mum's car. "You haven't learnt how to ride a bike yet and you may fall off and hurt yourself."

"Don't worry," I replied, knowing full well that I would want to have a go at riding it. And sure enough I had hardly sat on the saddle when I fell off! I knew straight away I had hurt my right arm as it felt sore and painful, but I didn't make a fuss because I thought Mummy would be cross with me. When we arrived home Mummy immediately saw my arm was badly broken near my elbow. Fortunately she wasn't cross and she and Daddy took me to casualty where my arm was re-set under an anaesthetic and plastered for six weeks.

Since my adoption I had suffered from nightmares which would leave me frightened and alone when I woke up, but on this particular night, while my arm was still in plaster, it was a completely different dream. I dreamt I was at school and having been to the toilet was washing my hands. In front of me was a large mirror. As I looked into the mirror I saw Jesus dressed in His white robes.

"How did you break your arm?" he asked.

"I fell off a bicycle," I replied and then He disappeared.

The next morning when I woke up I felt strangely comforted. How did I know it was Jesus? After all He would have known how I had broken my arm, so why ask me? I just knew it was Jesus and He had come to let me know that He loved and cared for me and was concerned about my accident. So perhaps I wasn't alone after all and that God and His son, Jesus, who Mummy talked about when she tucked me up in bed at night and taught me to say my prayers, really did exist. Perhaps I wasn't walking on that 'beach' on my own? But if Jesus cared about my broken arm, why had He allowed me to be separated from Mum? It was all rather confusing.

Life revolved around school, surgery times and playing with Marg, Liz and Brenda during the school holidays, then when I was seven years old and we moved to another house nearby I began to feel more secure, the daughter of my new parents, and so form happy memories that would last. One night when Mummy had tucked me up and said 'good night' with a kiss, I plucked up courage to ask, "What happened to my real Mum?"

Mummy sat on the bed and held my hand, "Your birth father died during the War, and soon afterwards your Mum remarried and went to live abroad. So your sister and brother were half-siblings. When you are older I will tell you more. In the meantime try to be the kind of daughter your birth father would be proud of. Does that answer your question?"

"Yes, thank you," and with that Mummy kissed me again and went downstairs.

So the man I had called Dad wasn't my real father. It was such a relief. Now I was beginning to understand why I looked so different from Tina and Chris and why Dad had hated me so much – I wasn't his child. I felt very proud that my real Dad had died fighting for his country and I would try to be a good daughter for him. But in less than five years I had had three fathers and two mothers.

So how did God, my Heavenly Father, and Jesus, who I had talked to in a dream, fit into all this? Was God my fourth father? Was He like my step-father or my real Dad or my adopted Daddy? It was all so confusing that the only thing I could do was to put God away in a 'box' until He showed me which Father He was. Jesus was there somewhere, but the best thing I could do for now was to remain strong for myself.

It was only a year later however, when my security collapsed again. Mummy told me that she and Daddy thought it would be good for me to go to a boarding school, so I didn't feel so lonely and had other children to play with. This was all very strange as I was perfectly happy with my life now and used to being an 'only' child. So why did they not want me around anymore? What had I done wrong? Why were they sending me away? I didn't like to question them as it occurred to me that if I did I might find myself with some different 'parents' again.

The school, a former stately home, was situated in the countryside about an hour away from Winchester, and something akin to Victorian school days. From day one I hated the school so was always being punished for some misdemeanour or other and especially for talking after 'lights out'. If you walked around with your hands in your coat pockets you had to sew the pockets up. Another punishment was walking round a large circular area of grass situated outside the headmistress's study. From here she could observe you and shout out if you were not walking fast enough. Ten times round was a mile and I seemed to walk miles!

Often I found it difficult to go to sleep at night, so I would look out of the window, watching the stars, and with tears in my eyes, start questioning God.

"Why did you let my real Dad die in the war and leave me all alone? I should be living with my proper Dad and Mum and not in this horrible place. Why did You let this happen to me and leave me so alone and unhappy. Why don't You help me?"

But there was no reply. I was trying so hard to be the daughter my birth father would have been proud of, but it was very difficult when I was so unhappy and no one seemed to love or even care about me and it wasn't easy trying to make new friends again. And what sort of daughter would he have wanted anyway? Life was still so complicated and I hated feeling so angry and lonely at times.

CHAPTER 4

School Days

I will instruct you and teach you in the way you should go.
(Psalm 32:8)

After three terms, with great relief, my parents agreed that I could return to St Swithun's as a day girl. I quickly made new friends as well as seeing more of Liz, Marg and Brenda at weekends and holidays and my life once again felt more secure. Then when I was eleven years old and had moved up into the Senior School I asked my parents if I could try boarding again and so became a border in one of the Junior Houses, Chilcomb.

This time I loved it – it was like living in one big happy family. Going to church on a Sunday was compulsory and a novelty to me as my parents very rarely went. We would walk down to St Thomas's church at the bottom of the hill wearing our school uniform, complete with hat and gloves and sit in rows in the church. I soon learnt the Matins service off by heart and loved singing the hymns, but I never really thought about what it all meant and at times it was rather boring, so

God remained in His 'box'. Life was going well now and I didn't need Him.

For special services we went to the Cathedral which I found so awe inspiring and wonderful. Every Remembrance Service I would remember my real Dad and join in the powerful hymns 'O God our help in Ages Past' and 'Jerusalem'. Then when the two minutes silence and the 'Last Post' was played by the trumpeters I would cry silently. I so much wanted to know what kind of man he had been. I had to hide my tears though because none of my friends knew I was adopted except for Mary.

Mary was my best friend and she encouraged me to ask my parents again about my adoption and so we rehearsed, on many occasions, how I would start the conversation. I was twelve years old at that time. In the end I chose to ask Daddy when he was taking me back to Chilcomb after an exeat.

"Daddy what happened to my real father?"

"Mummy and I have been waiting for you to ask us again," he replied. "You remember Mummy told you your real father had died in the war?"

"Yes," I replied.

"I think it would be better if Mummy told you the whole story, is that all right?"

"Yes."

Then he finally asked me if I was happy being with them so I assured him I was. We had now reached Chilcomb, so we said a swift 'goodbye' and I waited to hear the full story from Mummy.

It came in a letter a few days later.

'Darling Wendy,

Daddy tells me that you were asking him some questions about your parents. If you remember, you asked me some years ago, when you were quite small about your coming to live here with us, and I said that I would explain when you were old enough to understand. I have been expecting you to ask me about it for some time. I am writing this letter to you as I feel you must be worrying about it.

As you perhaps know, during the last war many people lost their lives through enemy action – lots of children lost one or both parents. This meant there were thousands of children needing new homes and new parents (these parents are called Adopters or Foster Parents). As Daddy told you yesterday, your real father was killed during the war. Your mother married again, so the man you thought was your real father was actually only your step-father. The children Tina and Christopher were your step-brother and sister. I expect you also remember that your step-father was not always very kind to you (because you were not his child). He took a post abroad when you came to us and your mother and the children went with him. I do not know where they are now.

As you know, Daddy and I have been happy together for many years. It was a great grief to us that we had no children of our own, so we were overjoyed that we were able to adopt you as our daughter.

I do want you to remember with affection and pride your real Daddy – he was in the Navy and was a very brave man. Always try to be the sort of daughter he would be proud of, if he had lived to see you.

Now don't worry about this matter again dear. When you write on Sunday next do tell me that you are happy and understand now – Daddy and I want you to have a happy life with us.

With love from us all

Mummy'

So I still didn't really know any more and knew I wouldn't learn the whole truth until I met Mum again, if ever.

Enclosed with the letter were five photographs of me as a baby and small child, which I treasured and put safely away in a drawer with the letter. It was so strange to think that I was that child and when they were taken I was still with Mum. And where were they taken? But for the moment I was content to enjoy my life as it was.

Soon after the letter, however, I let someone come too close to me, mainly because I was lonely during the holidays when my friends were not around to play with. Friends of my parents who lived across the road and who had no children they would take me sailing with them and often include me in various outings. I knew I would be made welcome and given some quality time. However, when his wife was out, her husband started to take advantage of this and when he gave me a hug would touch me in places that didn't seem right. It left me with a feeling of disgust and disappointment that someone I trusted was doing this to me. So I made sure I never got too close to him and only visited when his wife was there. I never told anyone, perhaps because like my adoption, the only way I could cope was to suppress my feelings and blot it all out – it hadn't happened to me. So the walls quickly built up around me again. It was not worth taking risks in trusting anyone but my parents again.

I had experienced so many changes in my short life that it came as no surprise when one day shortly after my 14th birthday my house mistress called me into her study. I had now moved into a senior boarding house.

"I am sorry to tell you," she said, "but your father had been taken ill, so I am allowing you to go home and see him this weekend."

I went home and Mummy told me Daddy had had a breakdown, owing to working too hard, and he was going to have to retire early. We would be moving to Sussex where we went twice a year for holidays to see Mummy's old friend, Aunty Mary. For the past few years we had stayed in a cottage on the edge of woods near the Downs and now we were going to live there until Daddy was better.

"Unfortunately," Mummy told me "we will not be able to continue to keep you at St Swithun's and you will have to go to a day school in Eastbourne at the beginning of next year. It will take us that time to sell the practice and the house."

Daddy looked so tired and grey that I was willing to do anything to see him return to his old self. I had been so busy with my life that I hadn't noticed how ill he was.

However before the move I was going to be confirmed in Winchester Cathedral. The previous year I had begun confirmation classes, given by Canon Lloyd who was the School Chaplain. He was very academic and I never understood anything he talked about, especially about the Holy Spirit. I knew about Jesus' birth and death, but no one had encouraged me to read my bible and I really wasn't very interested in learning more when it was too complicated to understand. So I would switch-off and worry about the fact that I was the only member of our group who had not been able to produce evidence of my baptism. I realised I must have been baptised otherwise my parents would not have let me be confirmed, but I didn't know and I didn't have the courage to ask them.

In March that year I went ahead with my confirmation in Winchester Cathedral because most of my friends were being confirmed. When the Bishop laid his hands on me all I could think of was whether my veil would stay on my head when I knelt down, as we had all had to wash our hair the evening before, which had made it shiny and slippery. God did not feature in this event. The following day when I went back to the Cathedral to take my first communion I felt so ill. Somehow I managed to get through the service and struggle home where I collapsed into Mummy's arms. I had Asian Flu – the flu that was to be one of the worst epidemics of the last half of the twentieth century. I was soon put to bed and stayed there until I was better, by which time school had closed early for the Easter Holidays as so many teachers and children were ill.

Later on that year, my parents moved to our new home and I joined them at the end of the autumn term. Gatewood was a small two-up, two-down cottage with no electricity, or running water and had an outside closet toilet. After a while Daddy set up a windmill to run a generator for electricity. This was not always sufficient to run a television, so he added a motor to the generator for when the wind was not blowing hard enough. Sometimes we would be watching some exciting sports programme or drama and the picture would get smaller and smaller, which meant Daddy had to rush outside and start the motor to the generator again so the picture would return! We stayed there a year, by which time Daddy was well enough to do locum work and we then moved to a house in the country near Hailsham.

So January the following year saw me getting onto a bus and going to a new school, St. Helena's in Eastbourne. I soon settled down and made plenty of friends. Fortunately for me it was not an academic school so I was able to choose the subjects I was most interested in for 'O' levels – Religious Education did not feature in my interests. I did not feel it was right to be examined on the bible. It would be like opening Pandora's Box and discovering things about God I did not like. He was safer left in His 'box' and not to be questioned about in an exam.

Hilary became a life-long friend and encouraged me to go to church with her on Sundays but once again it did not really mean anything to me. I enjoyed singing the hymns, found I could not understand the sermons, and the prayers, because I knew them off by heart, were said without any thought. Church was a way of filling a Sunday morning which would otherwise have been spent being bored and lonely. But on the whole I was happy enjoying my life.

CHAPTER 5

Marriage and Family

It is often by looking back on our lives that we see how God has given us light on our way through hard times and taught us things we would not otherwise have learnt.[3]

It wasn't long before the first prediction of the fortune teller came true and I received my 'O' level results in a brown envelope. Fortunately I passed enough to get me started on a career, although even after three attempts at Maths I never did pass it! I tried a number of jobs and careers after I left school but never felt they were right for me. Finally I went back to Winchester for six months and completed a secretarial course, the last thing I wanted to do, but something I knew would always stand me in good stead.

One of the jobs I had was spending a couple of terms as an assistant matron at a boys' prep school in Dorset, and there I met my future husband, Michael. He had been filling in time between bar exams and came to teach for one term. I felt flattered that this tall, attractive man with fair hair, who had been to Eton and was training to be a barrister, could be interested in me, someone who was short, not pretty or

---

[3] Coventry Cathedral leaflet 1989. See End notes.

attractive, and did not have his intellect. And I was sure he must be the man that Aunty Mary had seen in her tarot cards. Matron was unhappy about our relationship and told me 'there were plenty of other fish in the sea'. But as far as I was concerned here was a man I loved, who appeared to love me and could give me what I longed for – a family of my own.

So on a blustery sunny day in October 1967 Michael and I were married at my parents' local church, St Peter & St Paul's, Hellingly, Sussex, with Marg and Hilary as my bridesmaids. Daddy was anxious that we would be late getting to the church, but we were early and I saw Michael coming out of the pub, where he had been gathering up his family. It flashed through my mind that it was considered unlucky to see your future husband on the day of your marriage until you had stepped inside the church. And I also remembered the fortune-teller's prediction. But I quickly put all thoughts away as I stepped out of the car and walked down the aisle on my father's arm to Bach's Toccata and Fugue in D Minor. I was so happy when we said our vows to each other. I was going to spend the rest of my life with Michael and we would grow old together. The reception was held in a marquee in the garden of my parents' home and we then went to Somerset for a week before moving into our new home in Hassocks in Sussex.

The first few years of marriage were happy and we enjoyed setting up our home. Two years later our first child, Louise, was born followed by Mary two years after that. I soon discovered what a joy motherhood is – how had my birth mother been able to give me up?

However at times small problems began to arise in our marriage, especially concerning money. Michael had grown up in a family where money was in short supply and was a constant worry to his parents. I had grown up with parents who gave me what I wanted, because they showed their love for me in this way. So I waited for the difficult times to pass and the good times to come again and on the whole we were happy.

When I was pregnant with our third child, Michael felt it was time to move on and having changed careers to become a solicitor, accepted a job in Plymouth. Our move to a small village on the edge of Dartmoor took place in April 1976, and much to our delight a third daughter arrived the following month – Jane.

Within a few hours of Jane's birth I was struck by her likeness to Brenda, my childhood friend, but it soon passed and she began to resemble her two sisters when they were born. A little while later I became aware of Jane's stomach making funny noises like the central heating gurgling, but when I asked our GP he assured me there was nothing wrong with her. And sure enough the sounds soon disappeared.

However in mid-September Jane began vomiting more than normal. I took her to our doctor's surgery, but was told there was nothing wrong with her and to give her water to drink. The sickness continued during the evening, but on ringing the doctor was given the same advice. We moved Jane into our bedroom so I could keep an eye on her. She seemed to settle for a while then about 2 o'clock, she vomited again and this time it had black particles in it – dried blood I learnt later. Once again she settled after I had given her some water and so left her to sleep not wanting to call our GP out in the middle of the night. Finally at 6 o'clock when she vomited once more with more black particles in it, I knew something was seriously wrong with her and rung our GP.

"Jane is still vomiting, now with black particles in it, what do I do?" I said.

"Nothing, I am coming over now," she said. As soon as she had examined Jane she said, "I believe she has a volvulus of the stomach and she must go to hospital straight away."

I had no idea what a volvulus of the stomach was, but it sounded serious, so we left Louise and Mary with a neighbour and Michael and I quickly drove Jane to the hospital in Plymouth where she was operated on within a few hours. I felt so frightened giving Jane up to strangers, not knowing whether I would see her alive again. Who were these doctors and nurses, were they competent, did they know what they were doing, how could I leave my daughter with these people and not protect her myself? She was so small and defenceless. I should be taking care of her.

How would I cope if I lost her? I started to feel numb. I needed to blot out all feelings in order to remain strong – just as I had done as a small child. It was too difficult to comprehend that this was happening to my child and not someone else's. Somehow I had to draw on all my inner strength to cope with this. But I also knew deep down I couldn't do it on my own. I needed to turn to God because I couldn't make Jane better on my own. I had to let Him out of His 'box' for a short time.

We were told it would be some time before she came back to the ward and more or less told to leave, so we went to Michael's office, which was nearby. I sat on a window seat and silently prayed and prayed God would make her well again. As I looked out of the window people were still getting on with their lives, but somehow mine had stopped, as though I was in a time warp. Michael and I hardly spoke to each other, but both realised it would be easier if we did something to take our minds off the operation.

"Let's go and look for some carpets for the cottage," Michael said. "There's a carpet shop nearby."

Looking back it seemed a strange thing to do, but we had never been in that situation before, so to do something normal seemed the best way to cope. When we returned to the hospital Jane was back in her cot on the ward and looking so much better. God had heard my prayers.

"The operation went well," Jane's paediatrician told us, "but the surgeon was only able to do an emergency operation to save her life. Because of a hole in her diaphragm, her stomach had had too much room to move around and it became twisted. She will need to have further surgery to repair the hole in her diaphragm at a later date. This will have to be done in Bristol."

Jane stayed in hospital for five days and for the next few weeks I was constantly worried as she continued to be sick at times. Finally in early October our doctor had her readmitted to hospital where she was referred to the Bristol Children's Hospital. So once again I watched Jane being carried by a nurse to the operating theatre and constantly praying for her to return to her cot safe and well. Somehow this time it wasn't quite so difficult. God had heard my prayers the first time so I knew He would hear them this time too.

It was several hours before she returned and moved into Intensive Care, where she was attached to various monitors and a chest drain. What struck me most was how pink and well she looked, as right from her birth she had been so pale. The operation was successful and Jane was only in Intensive Care for a few days and then returned to the general ward. Michael came up with Louise and Mary for the day the following weekend and we went to Bristol Zoo. It was lovely seeing the family again and for a few hours to live a more normal life.

While I was waiting for Jane to be discharged a 'watershed' moment took place. Although looking back now it seemed such an insignificant moment, but at the time I knew then that my marriage would not last. Our expectations of each other seemed to be poles apart at times. One evening feeling particularly lonely I decided to ring Michael for a chat. With little money on me I rang to reverse the call, but he refused to pay for it as he later said he had nothing to tell me. I felt devastated and hurt. Why had he done this when I needed someone to talk to?

However, I had three small children to bring up in a family atmosphere, so somehow I must make my marriage work for the next few years. I wasn't going to seek help or discuss the matter with anyone, especially Michael. I knew my marriage was not going to work because the fortune-teller had told me so. God did not feature in any decisions I might make in the future. As far as I was concerned it was up to me to fight any battles that lay ahead. Once again I saw myself walking alone on that dark sandy beach and God was firmly back in His 'box'.

Jane spent two weeks in hospital and during this time I noticed her feet were a strange shape compared with the other babies. So a few weeks later we were referred to an orthopaedic consultant in Plymouth, who told us Jane's feet were fine, but both her hips were dislocated – she had been born with Congenital Dislocation of the Hips (CDH). Arrangements were then made for her to be admitted to the orthopaedic hospital after Christmas for six weeks in traction. It was so difficult leaving her on her own at night. I would ring up before I went to bed and be told she was fine, but the following morning when I returned other mothers, who had been able to stay overnight, would tell me she had cried herself to sleep. Why God, why, does Jane have to suffer like this? But once again God was silent to my cries.

Jane was in traction for six weeks and then at home in plaster for several months while the doctors tried to get her hips to stay in place, but finally her left hip had to be operated on. Less than a week after she came out of plaster and was wearing a special brace, she slipped off a small wooden push-bike and broke the femur of her right leg. So she was put back into plaster. It was quite a year.

The following June Jane had a further operation this time on her right hip with another six weeks again in plaster. She was 2 years and 5 months old when she started walking for the first time – a wonderful occasion!

By 1979 we had all settled down to a mainly happy life, with Michael and me only having the odd argument. Michael had set up his own practice, Louise and Mary both happy in our local village school and Jane now attended a nursery school. I made more friends and life was busy with coffee mornings, supper parties, school and church activities to attend or help with.

We had got to know our Rector well through Jane being in hospital and prayers being said for her in church. With Louise and Mary in the choir, Michael and I went more often to church, taking Jane with us, but it really became a time of planning the week ahead and not a time of worship and growing closer to God. I became Clerk to the Governors of their school and went on the Parochial Church Council. The following year I was asked if I would edit the church magazine – a job I did for many years and thoroughly enjoyed.

Jane had further surgery on her left hip when she was three which was successful this time. Then when she was five years old we were told her right hip needed further surgery. This came as a blow because she had had no problems walking on the moors for long distances with her father and didn't appear to be in any pain. So I took her to Great Ormond Street Hospital for a second opinion, which confirmed the diagnosis. A few months later Jane was operated on in Plymouth.

By this time Jane was becoming more aware of what was happening, but she never complained and seemed to accept that somehow what she went through would make her better. And once again I found myself juggling family and visits to the hospital, with the help of family and friends. And to let God out of His 'box' for a short time for His help and support.

In hindsight I wish we had said "no" to any more operations, but somehow you find you have to trust the doctors and go along with what they say, because you believe they know better than you do – in those days there was no internet to go to to get more information. Her hip had had to be reconstructed and pinned, but following the operation, Jane developed an infection in the wound and became very ill, bringing up about a pint of bile every time she had anything to eat or drink.

I took her back to hospital where she had to have the pin removed, which made her hip less stable, and another plaster cast was put on. I then told the medical staff that I would not have her home until she was no longer vomiting – I just could not cope any more seeing my child in so much distress and needed more support. Michael always seemed so busy running his practice, so I never really felt I had a great deal of support from him. Now I realise I was probably shutting him out and was trying to cope on my own as I had always done.

My friends were a wonderful help to me and when Jane was home again her nursery school didn't mind having her there in her plaster cast. I managed to buy a second-hand twin pushchair and she was happy to sit in this and join in with what she could. Finally in August the plaster was removed and in September she joined Louise and Mary who were now in a school in Plymouth, although she was unable to walk unaided for some time. Fortunately the staff were very understanding and with physiotherapy she started to walk again.

However the operation was not successful, leaving Jane with an unstable hip joint which would in time need a hip replacement. We later learnt that this particular procedure was stopped as many children had never been able to walk again and were confined to a wheelchair.

CHAPTER 6
Difficult Times

*Take my yoke upon you and learn from me, for I am gentle
and humble in heart, and you will find rest for your souls.
(Matt. 11:29)*

The next three years went by quickly with the girls becoming
involved in Pony Club activities, each one having their own
pony. Louise and Mary also played a lot of sport and Jane was
able to ride and swim. Summer holidays were spent in
Cornwall. In 1984 we moved to a larger house in the same
village, with a paddock for the ponies – the large white house
that the fortune teller had predicted those many years before.
This just left meeting my birth mother again – I was still
determined to find her – and then all the four predictions
would have come true. So perhaps I was going to see her again
after all.

Jane's walking however was not improving and she had
now developed a 'drop foot' on her right leg, so I took her
back to see her paediatrician. After a long discussion about
what had happened after Jane's last hip operation, he said,

"I believe that her sciatic nerve has been badly damaged causing her foot to drop. She will need to see a different consultant to see what can be done."

This led to Jane being referred to yet another consultant in 1985, this time at St Mary's Hospital, in London and having a tendon transplant done on her foot, to prevent the foot dropping even further. And it did help a little. However by now her right hip had formed its own socket causing her leg to be shorter than her left. So over the next seven years she was to have five operations on her left leg so it didn't grow too long, all followed by six to eight weeks in plaster. She had a wonderful surgeon, David Hunt, and a great deal of progress was made, but she was to remain in constant pain and need the use of a walking stick.

Throughout all her surgery, Jane still managed to remain stoical and would comment on how much worse off some of the other children on the ward were, and that she was thankful that something could be done for her. It is as though God gives children like Jane a very special gift – an inner strength to cope with all that is being done to them; an ability to be able to accept what is going on in their lives, especially being in a difficult environment amongst strangers and above all to bear the terrible pain some of them have to suffer. They are all incredibly brave. They also develop a great compassion and understanding of other people's suffering.

I remember one particular occasion when Jane was in St Mary's for the second time, a child younger than her coming in late one evening with a broken arm following a road accident. She was very frightened, in pain and hysterical and there seemed nothing that her mother or the staff could do to comfort her. I had to leave Jane soon afterwards, and the next day when I came in the girl seemed happier and more accepting as to what had happened.

"How's the little girl doing across from you?" I asked Jane.

"Oh I went to see her after you had gone and I told her about me and all the times I had been in hospital and somehow that helped."

I just felt so overwhelmed that my daughter at the age of ten was able to go and minister to a child younger than her who was frightened and in pain.

I stayed with some wonderful friends, Tim and Rosemary, who would ferry me to and from the hospital each day and have a meal waiting for me in the evening. I cannot recall Michael ever coming to London to see Jane, as he felt he could not leave his work. So each time she was operated on I was left on my own to wait until her return from the operating theatre. But then why did I need anyone? I was strong. I had always had to be and always would have to be. God was there if I needed Him to pray to when Jane went down to theatre. And after all the church was praying for her too, so that must be enough.

1985 turned out to be a terrible year. While Jane was recovering from her operation a different doctor checking on her progress said, "So this is the Marfan patient?"

I just nodded my head as I had no idea what Marfan was and thought it must be something to do with hips and thought nothing more about it.

Jane hadn't been home very long before I received unexpected news from Daddy telling me Mummy had died from a heart attack. She had been in hospital in Chichester for a week or so, as he hadn't been able to cope any longer looking after her, as she had developed Parkinson's disease. As I had been taking care of Jane I hadn't been able to go up and see her and Daddy also hadn't indicated her condition was so serious. I immediately left the girls – Jane was still in plaster – with a close friend, Sheila, and went up to Sussex to be with Daddy and help him make the funeral arrangements. Michael joined us for the funeral. I was sad Mummy had died, but did not feel a great sense of loss as I had never really felt close to her. Daddy then came to live with us a short while later and for the first time I had him to myself and could really appreciate the wonderful person he was. He also enjoyed having his grandchildren around him and watching them growing up.

Yet worse was still to come. The month following Mummy's death Olive, the mother of my childhood friend, Brenda, came to stay for a few days. Brenda had died ten years before at the age of 31. She had had a valve replacement done on her aorta and finally the aorta had ruptured in another place. One afternoon Olive and I went for a walk and I was telling her about Jane's operation. Quite casually and I do not know why I did, I said,

"One of the doctors mentioned something about Jane having Marfan."

Olive's reply numbed me. "But that is what Brenda died from."

How strange that I had noticed the similarity to Brenda when Jane was born. Somehow God had prepared me for this moment, but all I could think of was that Jane could die at an early age. On our return home I immediately rang Michael who told me to make an appointment to see our doctor and this was followed by a visit to a cardiology consultant. The size of her aorta, together with other indicators, would confirm she had the condition, and they did. Marfan Syndrome is described as 'a variable disorder of the connective tissues and can affect the eyes, skeleton, lungs, heart and blood vessels and can be life threatening'.

It seemed so unfair that Jane was going through so much at such a young age. I can't remember Michael and I ever sitting down together to discuss Jane's condition and how it could affect the whole family, but I do remember we did agree that we would never prevent her from doing what she felt capable of doing. A good quality of life was more important than quantity. So I would take each day at a time, trying to keep everything as normal for the children and Michael, and not worry that Jane had a life threatening condition. Somehow I just knew that God was taking care of her because maybe, just maybe, He needed her for a special purpose.

The following year the whole family went to St. George's Hospital in London to meet Dr Anne Child, a clinical geneticist who was heavily involved in research into Marfan Syndrome. We were all examined in order to see if the gene was travelling through the family which it wasn't. Jane belonged to the 25% of spontaneous cases. There is then a 50-50 chance of passing it on. The faulty gene was finally discovered in 1990 and in 1991 a deficiency was found in the glycoprotein, 'fibrillin'. Tests showed that Jane's aorta was stretched, but with regular monitoring and beta blockers to slow her heart rate down it is kept under control. Thankfully with all the research that is now being done, Jane stands a much better chance of living for a longer time than Brenda did, although it is still a life threatening condition.

I found the whole visit very difficult for me because I had no idea about my own medical background and had to explain I was adopted. For some reason it always gave me a sense of 'aloneness' not knowing anything about my natural parents, whether I had inherited anything I did not know about. It came out later that during that visit Mary had discovered I had been adopted and could not understand why I had never discussed it with her and her sisters until after my father's death. Once again I was trying to shield my adopted parents.

Finally Dr Childs told us about the Marfan Association[4] which had been formed the previous year and from them we learnt more about the condition and kept informed of any new research. Some years later Jane, Michael and I attended an Information Day. It was interesting to meet so many people with Marfan and to hear how they coped.

Jane attended one of these Information Days on her own when she was 19 years old and was asked if she would mind telling her story for an article in the teenage girls' magazine, *MIZZ*. The reporter had decided to use this as one of three conditions which some teenagers live with, the other two being muscular dystrophy and cystic fibrosis.

When the article appeared I was shocked to see on the cover the words 'Living with a killer – Too young to die – Teenagers fighting fatal diseases'. Although I knew Marfan could be fatal because Brenda had died from the condition, I found it difficult to associate these stark words with my own daughter. The article concentrated on how Jane sees herself and how she lives with Marfan. Having tried to make sure she lives her life to the full and does not allow herself to be limited by Marfan, I found the contents quite revealing as it wasn't something we talked about very often. Presented as though it were a direct quotation – it is in fact rewritten from what Jane actually said – this is how her story was put across:

---

[4] See Useful Addresses.

"I was born with dislocated hips and have to walk with a stick. I had to have loads of operations as a baby, but it wasn't until I was nine that I was diagnosed as having Marfan Syndrome. Nobody actually told me, though – I found out by accident. I was in hospital and a medical student came in and asked, 'Is this the girl with Marfan Syndrome?' Most people have never heard of the condition, so the doctors must have assumed I wouldn't have picked up on it. It's normally passed on from a parent, but sometimes it occurs spontaneously, and that's what happened with me.

Mum knew all about it, because she'd had a friend who died from the condition at the age of 30. Funnily enough, when I was born Mum was struck at how much I looked like her friend. The disorder affects the skeleton, so people affected are very tall, with long fingers. The doctors didn't handle it brilliantly at first, and were quite evasive, but luckily my Mum was still in touch with her friend's Mum and found out more about it through her.

It wasn't a huge shock to me, because I already knew that I was different because of my hips. But now I knew the reason why – the gene that dealt with the connective tissue was faulty and my bones weren't being given the right genetic message, causing them to grow long and dislocated. More worryingly, my heart was weakened, although since my diagnosis I get regular check-ups and seem to be okay.

I don't really think about it, but whenever I tell my friends they seem to get a bit upset for me. I think people always associate genetic disorders as being quite serious. I used to worry a bit myself, but going to the Marfan Association and meeting other sufferers has made me realise that I'm not alone. Although young children always stare, because of my limp and my stick, I get a sympathetic reaction from most people. There have only been a few occasions which have upset me. I was working as a counsellor on a kids' summer camp, and this girl, another worker, had been sent to find me. I was wearing shorts, which is quite a big deal for me because my legs are ultra-thin and very scarred from operations. When she saw me, she couldn't hide her disgust. Later, whenever she spoke to me, she kept going on about how my legs looked. Thankfully, people like her are quite rare.

Obviously, Marfan Syndrome affects the way I look, and my self-image is quite low. Every so often, I have a huge crisis about it, but it hasn't affected my ability to get boyfriends – although it always surprises me when I do! In some ways it's an advantage to know that they're with me for me, as opposed to my looks.

I do worry about having children. I have a one in two chance of passing on the gene, and it's hard to know how serious the condition will be in future generations. There are pre-natal tests, but there's also my health to worry about. Having a baby might not be the best thing for my hips and heart condition. I've got a lot of thinking to do on the subject.

I don't want to make a huge deal about having Marfan Syndrome, but I'm talking to *MIZZ* because the majority of families with the condition only discover that they're affected when one of them dies of it. That's a real shame, because there's a lot that can be done to help people, but without treatment the average age of death is 32. I sometimes see people on the street who are very tall and with long fingers, and think 'Do you have Marfan Syndrome and not know about it?' So even if there's only one person reading this who has the condition but is undiagnosed and gets themselves checked out, it will have all been worth it."[5]

So the years passed revolving mainly around Jane's operations. My father offered to pay for us to have family holidays overseas which were a great success. One year we went to Cayman Brac in the Caribbean and met Erin Pizzey who was living on the island at the time, and we soon got to know her quite well. Having founded the first refuge for battered wives in 1971 in Chiswick, West London, sometime later I was interested to watch a television documentary about these refuges. It was a revelation for me. One of the women interviewed, who came from a similar background to mine, told how her husband had treated her and the way he would speak to her. Suddenly I realised this was how Michael was treating me and how he spoke to me at times – I had not realised it wasn't the right way to behave. When this lady entered the refuge, Erin told her that mental abuse was far worse than physical abuse – 'it wears the abused person down, makes them lose all their self-esteem and gives them the impression they are useless'.

For a long time I hadn't understood why Michael was so critical of me at times and feelings of self-pity would then surface. After all I cooked, washed, cleaned the house, did the shopping and looked after the girls and loved him – what else did he want from me? His comments would often undermine my confidence and make me feel small. My friends seemed to accept me for who I was. So why was my ability to do things I knew I couldn't do well matter so much – surely doing something to the best of your ability, was more important?

---

[5] *Mizz*. (London IPC Magazine Issue 291. 22 May – 4 June 1996), p 60.

Many times after we had had an argument and Michael would not speak to me, I would remember my 'dream beach'. I cried a great deal during those lonely nights, but somehow the knowledge that my three daughters needed me kept me going. I also needed to learn to lean on God more during these difficult times. When I was feeling low, I would lie in the bath sing Psalm 23, 'The Lord is my Shepherd', and somehow this helped. But I was so angry with God. Haven't I gone through enough with Mum giving me up, Jane's health, and now I was married to a man who doesn't seem to love me?

I never told anyone what I was going through though as I did not want to put Michael down. For some reason he could not accept me for the person I was. But then I had lost my identity when I was adopted and for years had to be whoever the people I was with wanted me to be, so I didn't really know who I was anyway.

CHAPTER 7

Adoption Investigated

I will repay you for the years the locusts have eaten.
(Joel 2: 25a)

Time moved on with its usual ups and downs and as the 1980s came to a close tremendous changes came into our lives. It was also the time I discovered my roots and the final prediction the fortune-teller had made came true.

Early in 1989 Jane started confirmation classes with one of the team ministers, Geoff Ball, and was confirmed at Yelverton Church, which began a chain of events that were going to bring about changes in my life that I could never have imagined.

Michael then decided he would like to spend a year at Cambridge University reading for an M.Phil and was subsequently accepted at Wolfson College.

When he first decided to go to Cambridge, I was quite prepared to remain in Devon, but after more thought I decided to join him returning home during the holidays. Perhaps by being together in a different environment we would be able to sort out our marriage and make a fresh start.

Michael and I soon settled into college life. We attended Formal Hall, where I found I was talking to people from many different parts of the world, some being eminent figures in their field and I soon learnt to listen and look intelligent, even if I did not understand much of what I was being told! We also attended concerts and rugby matches and regularly went to Evensong at Trinity College Chapel. These services were wonderful, but it was the music I went to hear, rather than to worship God – once again the words were so familiar that I recited or sang them while thinking of other things and the sermons were often far above my head.

Then much to my amazement I was offered two secretarial jobs in the University and accepted the one working for the Cambridge Philosophical Society, which included helping to edit the two journals the Society produced, Mathematical Proceedings and Biological Reviews.

However during the first three months we were there, both Michael's parents died within a few weeks of each other. Then in late January Daddy had a stroke and was taken into hospital in Plymouth – the same hospital where Jane had had her first orthopaedic surgery, and was now a geriatric hospital. In early March he had a second stroke and became unconscious. Michael and I went back to Plymouth straight away and I was told there was nothing more that could be done for him. So I asked the doctors to withdraw all treatment. It was an awful decision to make, but Daddy had been a doctor and would have understood the situation. He had had a good life and was now 86 years old and I knew he would not want to prolong his death in an unconscious state. He died five days later and the funeral was held in Sussex so he could be buried with my mother.

A few weeks later when I was sorting through his papers two interesting things came to light. Firstly I found a photograph taken of me in June 1949 by a photographer in Alton, which must have been for my adoption – an occasion I have no recollection of. Then as I was checking his bank statement I saw he had been paying an annual Banker's Order to NCAA for £1.10 – the old one guinea. I had kept an article from The Times following the change of law in 1976 giving adopted adults the right to access information concerning their birth and adoption. When I telephoned the help number I was told that the NCAA, The National Children's Adoption Association, was no longer in existence and that the City of Westminster held all their files.

The following month I wrote to them asking for their help in tracing my birth parents. By doing this I was well aware that my need to discover my roots could change the lives of many people and open up many memories that had been shut away for over forty years. I could also experience rejection again. But it was something I knew I had to do. I needed to find Mum.

I received a reply from the City of Westminster a few days later telling me that they had my records, but I would have to get in touch with my local Social Services Department to see a counsellor before they would release the file. It was another four weeks before I was told I could go and read my file.

"Are you still sure you want to read your file?" the counsellor asked me.

"Yes, of course," I replied.

"I have to warn you that the story you told me of your adoption doesn't fit in with what you will read in your file. You may find it upsetting."

"It doesn't matter." I replied. "I still want to read it whatever it has to tell me."

With that she handed over the file and left me on my own to read it. The green cover was starting to fade around the edges, but all the correspondence was in remarkably good condition considering its age. On the cover was the number of the file, my name and address as 'Godwin Wendy Gaye' and Alton, Hants, along with my birth date all in large letters and legalised on 27/3/1950. So I had recognised the house where I had lived with Mum all those years ago. As I opened the file the first letter came as a great shock. It had been written to the adoption association on the 10 July 1989 from a sister, Jenny Coates, living in Chelmsford, stating that she and other members of the family would like to find me. The next letter was from Social Services, City of Westminster, informing Mrs Coates that they now held my file and would put her letter on my file and 'should she ever get in touch would be only too pleased to make her aware of it... The number of people who ask for access to their records is however relatively small and the number who want to make contact with their birth family is even fewer.'

I couldn't take in this letter right now, so I quickly turned to the end of the file to start reading everything from the beginning.

The first letter was from my step-father requesting that the NCAA consider having me put up for adoption, which was followed by the reply that their Committee was prepared to consider the application after meeting Geoff. There are then notes written by hand on scraps of paper by a Mrs Ogg, the first of which read:

"After hearing his [Geoff's] story I am definitely of the opinion that the little girl should be adopted. Mr Godwin and his wife knew each other since childhood and while he was overseas he kept up correspondence with her – in 1944 he received a letter from her stating she was expecting a child to another man. He managed to return to England and they were married in July 1944. The child was born in the following January and there are now two other children. Mr Godwin has felt all along that he could not feel to this child in the same way as his own. He feels the other two children are becoming aware of the difference and this is not fair to his wife's child.

Two days later it would appear that Mum took me up to see Mrs Ogg as she wrote:

"Mrs Godwin called with Wendy – her little girl who is perfectly sweet. In my opinion a most intelligent child with lovely curly hair and good features. The Father was killed on 'D' Day – aged 20 and was in the Navy. He was a gentleman farmer, as his family have been for generations. They knew each other for four years and would have been married, but his family did not approve. Mrs Godwin very nice and a good family – her father is a doctor. This child is of good background."

Mum had completed the application form and it was here I discovered I was classed as 'illegitimate' – was that what the counsellor was concerned about? At this moment it didn't seem to matter. I saw that Geoff was recorded as my father on a copy of my birth certificate so that was fine by me. Mum was asked to supply two references – one from Dr Baker from Lyme Regis and the other someone Geoff knew. The Adoption Association needed to know how long the referee had known the applicant, Mrs P. Godwin, if she was a respectable girl previous to the birth of the child and whether, "should we be able to help her at the present time, you have reason to believe that she will lead a satisfactory life in the future?"

Dr Barker replied:

"Known since 1941 and to the best of my knowledge she was a perfectly respectable girl previous to the birth of the child. She comes of a good family and always seemed quiet and intelligent. As she is now married and has two other children, I can see no reason why her life in the future should not be satisfactory, provided, of course, she is quite certain in her own mind that the course she is taking in having Wendy adopted is the right one."

Obviously my 'illegitimacy' was of great concern at that time.

In 'A full description of the case' on the form Mum wrote:

"I first met the father in 1940. He was already serving with RN and his best friend and I were in the same class at the Lyme Regis Grammar School. After the father's return from leave we corresponded regularly, tho' not meeting from July 1941 to November 1943 when he was serving overseas. For the following five months we met regularly, while the father was stationed ashore at Devonport. In April 1944 we became engaged, tho' parents on both sides object, believing we were too young to think of marriage – I desire this adoption as Wendy is beginning to notice that she does not quite belong to our family – while her younger brother and sister are not very kind already feeling there is a difference between her and themselves. She needs a great deal of loving, of which I am afraid she does not get enough "

Within a few weeks Mum was informed that the NCAA had an 'excellent home in mind for your little girl and the adopters are anxious to see her on Wednesday 3rd August at 2.45pm with a view to taking her home with them'.

Mum wrote back confirming that she would bring me to the office, adding 'I shall bring her clothing etc. and hope that everything will be arranged satisfactorily'. So I should have had some clothes with me. I expect Geoff hadn't wanted to take a suitcase with us when I finally left Mum as I might have asked too many questions and refused to leave Mum again.

The next letter in the file was dated 31st August from Dr Barker of Lyme Regis (one of the referees) to Mrs Plummer the General Secretary of The National Children's Adoption Association.

"Mrs Godwin's mother, Mrs Underhill, who is a patient of mine, has recently learnt about the adoption of her grand-daughter, to whom she was devoted, and the news has been a very great shock to her. She is desperately, and understandably, anxious to hear what she can about the child's "fate" and I promised her that I would write to you for any details you may be able or willing to let her have. I told Mrs. Underhill that it would be unwise for her to attempt to see Wendy, at least for a very long time, as this would unsettle the child at a time when she is probably finding security for the first time; and she has agreed not to attempt to do so. I should be very grateful, however, for any details of Wendy's foster parents that you are allowed to supply, or at least some assurance of the child's well-being with which I can comfort my patient."

5th September – a reply from Mrs Plummer:

"I am very glad to give you the happiest news of Wendy Godwin, who has been adopted by a professional man and his wife; they are cultured and delightful people and Wendy is extremely happy with them. There would be no question of a relation being able to see the little girl now that she has gone to these people, but I could get a photograph a little later on which the grandmother might be allowed to see. We felt very sorry that this little girl could not remain with her mother, but the mother told me that she did not love her the same as she did her other children, and everything seemed to point that it would be in the best interests of Wendy to be adopted where she was really wanted."

What a shock that must have been for my grandmother. Why hadn't Mum told her? But then if she had known she might have wanted to have me live with her and then Geoff wouldn't have been rid of me.

The next letter was on the 9th December – a letter from Mrs Plummer written to Mum, at the Alton address, saying:

"I had settled down most happily with the adopting parents and they are devoted to her and she returns their love. The adopters wish to make the adoption legal without delay, so that they can make her future position secure."

Mum was then asked to go with Geoff to sign the High Court Consent Forms which they did on 16th December and so relinquishing any parental rights in the future.

Included in the file was a copy of my Baptismal Certificate stating I had been baptised on 29 May 1945 at Uplyme Parish Church, Lyme Regis. It was good to know that!

The case for my adoption was finally heard on 27th March and legalised on 6th May 1950. Malcolm, a family name of my adopted father, was then added to my Christian names.

Finally on 27th June there was a letter to Mum from NCAA saying:

"We are pleased to advise you that a full adoption order has been granted to the adopters who have Wendy; this means she is irrevocably in their care and neither you nor your husband has any further claim to the little girl. We assure you Wendy is making splendid progress in every way; she is much loved by her adopting parents and will have a happy upbringing with them. We would be glad to receive a letter signed by you and your husband to the effect you both understand the legal adoption has been completed."

Although it had only taken eight weeks, from the time of application to living with my new parents, Mum was still receiving letters about me one year after these proceedings had started. It is difficult to imagine how she must have felt during that time, and it would take me some time to really understand what she went through.

As I closed the file tears welled up in my eyes and I let them flow knowing I wouldn't be interrupted. After all these years I was beginning to know the truth about my adoption and most importantly how my birth father had died.

My sister Jenny's letter however, saying my natural family were trying to find me, placed me in a dilemma. Did I want to know any more and did I really want to meet Mum again after such a long time? Or more to the point did she really want to see me again?

CHAPTER 8

An Unexpected Reunion

'Taste and see that the Lord is good' (Psalm 34:8a)

It didn't take me long to make the decision to write to Jenny – after all they were looking for me as much as I wanted to find them. I received a reply by return:

"Our biggest fear was never finding out whether you were even alive, let alone where you were."

She went on to tell me all about Mum, my three half-brothers, Chris, Tony and Ken and two other half-sisters, Tina and Liz, all of whom were living in Canada, except for Chris who lived in Hong Kong. Tina was also living in the same town as Mum. Of Mum she wrote:

"Mum, usually known as Pen lives alone (except for her pets) in a small town about 150 miles from Winnipeg, called Neepawa. I have already called her to say I've heard from you and she is so pleased, but terribly apprehensive about how you will feel about her. She would love to contact you, but realises how difficult the situation is and will wait until you feel you would like to get in touch with her. She has never forgotten you, and has thought about you so often."

Jenny continued:

"Do you remember our Grandmother at all; apparently she doted on you, although I've never heard what her reaction was to your being sent away. She was known as 'Weena' [Edith Betty] and she died earlier this year aged 91. Mum, Tina and I went down to Lyme Regis to sort out her things and Mum showed us where you were born... Although Geoffrey Godwin was put on your birth certificate as Father, he was not. When Mum became pregnant with you her family would not allow her to marry your Father as he wasn't 'good enough'. Geoff and Mum had been friends so he offered to marry her. I don't know how long it was before Geoff turned against you but I do know he made your life a misery. Mum tried to leave him at one stage, but her father told her they would not help her at all. I only have very vague memories of him myself but have been told he was an extremely domineering man who ruled his household with a rod of iron. All the children lived in terror of him and it was for your protection Mum finally gave you up for adoption."

Like me, Jenny the youngest child, had not grown up with the rest of the family. Mum had been very ill after her birth and she had been looked after by the district midwife and had then remained with her and her husband until she left school. With the letter were photographs of various members of the family including several of Mum. It was strange looking at a picture of my birth mother – the last time I had seen her she was 22 and now she was 63 years old.

Since the family was overseas, I decided to ring Jenny to suggest a meeting and so she came up to Cambridge. We got on well and she filled in the missing years as much as she could, being my junior by twelve years, while I told her all about my life. Jenny had learnt of my existence when on a visit to Canada and with Mum being happy for Jenny to search for me had spent a day at St Catherine's House looking for my name in the Adoptions Register, but had not looked far enough ahead at the entries.

She told me that Geoff had given Mum a very difficult time during their marriage and had died over twenty years before. He had been a keen sailor and had crossed the Atlantic single-handed, after which he had decided to emigrate to Canada and so in 1965 he, Mum and Ken moved to Nova Scotia. A little while later Geoff returned to England to buy another boat, returning this time with a friend. After they had rounded Ireland they are believed to have both been lost at sea.

As we were returning from our walk Jenny dropped a 'bombshell'.

"I don't know how you will take this news," she said, "but I think you should know that your birth father did not die during the war and as far as Mum knows he is still alive. Mum returned to England every year to visit our grandmother in Lyme Regis and on one occasion she heard that, following a heart attack, he had returned to the town. His name is Sam Miller."

"Oh" I replied "I don't know if I can really take this in at the moment. When I started my search I only wanted to see Mum again. I'm not sure if I really want to find out any more about him. It has come as rather a shock. But thank you for telling me."

As we continued chatting, discovering lots of things we had in common, I knew I had to fly to Canada to meet Mum. I owed it to her and to myself to try to make more sense of the past. Mum had let Jenny know she would like to see me again, so if it did not work out – and apparently very few meetings of this kind do – at least I would not spend the rest of my life regretting that I had not gone.

I had to wait for three weeks before I could get a flight and on a Saturday in July I flew from Heathrow to Winnipeg, to meet my mother, my sister Tina and younger brother Ken. During the entire flight I tried to keep my mind blank about the forth-coming meeting – what would be would be. I can recall though praying to God that everything would go well and somehow I felt I was doing the right thing.

The flight went well and we landed at Winnipeg on time that same evening. By now my stomach was beginning to churn. How would I recognise Mum and how would I greet her? The airport at Winnipeg was small and when I reached the one and only carousel for collecting luggage, it had broken down. Finally the carousal started moving – only to stop a few minutes later! Eventually after several stops and starts I was able to claim my luggage, and go through the green doors to meet my mother after forty-one years.

However as soon as I was through the doors I was met by 'a sea of faces', standing mostly to my left – an impossible situation to pick out one person amongst so many. I then happened to glance to my right where a group of three women stood, one older than the other two.

"Mum?" I tentatively asked, and with a nod of her head I went forward and we hugged each other and cried. After all those years it seemed the most natural thing to do, although it also seemed strange to be hugging this grey-haired woman who was my mother and someone I could have passed in the street and not realised who she was. However, Mum told me later that she had immediately recognised me, as I looked so much like my father.

The other two women turned out to be my sister Tina and my brother Ken's wife, Janine, who both lived in Winnipeg. This involved more hugs and tears! With Janine pushing my luggage on a trolley, Mum, Tina and I, with our arms around one another, headed for the lift to take us to the airport café where we could sit down and start talking and getting to know each other, before leaving Jan in Winnipeg, and driving to Neepawa.

I only spent a week with Mum, but I had taken my adoption file with me and we were able to go through it together so she could fill in the gaps and to talk and talk getting to know each other again.

She told me that Geoff had dictated the Adoption Application Form for her to write. Most of it was lies to convince the Agency that he had a good case, but the story of meeting my father was correct. She also told me that after she had become engaged, Sam had been posted to HMS Owl for three months in the North of Scotland, on special duties, and could not get back to Lyme. Geoff, a Flight Sergeant in the RAF, had been stationed in Lyme Regis and had got to know Mum's family, but was not a particular friend of hers.

On discovering she was pregnant Mum's parents had made her break off her engagement as they felt Sam was not good enough for her and told her his parents did not want her to marry him either. So Mum wrote to Geoff, who was now stationed in Iceland, telling him what had happened. He had telegraphed back "Will you marry me?" My grandfather had waved it at her and said, "Do I send 'Yes', or will you go away until the baby is born and adopted?"

Mum was only 17 years old and had never been away from home and being afraid she said, 'Yes'.

So in July 1944 Mum married Geoff, in the Parish Church in Lyme Regis, and the following January I was born in my grandparent's house.

After Chris was born Mum had told her mother she was not happy and wanted to leave Geoff, but her father had told her 'she had made her bed and now she must lie on it'.

She described the day she took me to the Adoption Agency offices and how I was taken by a member of staff into another room where I was to wait for my adoptive parents to come and take me back to their home. But because I had been so hysterical when I left Mum, new arrangements had been made. As it had been for me, Mum had also found the whole procedure so traumatic that she could only remember some of the things that had taken place.

In many ways it was as though we had never been apart, but in others there had been too many years separating us – too many gaps which could never been filled.

One of the most amazing things I discovered was that when I had spent my first Christmas with Michael's family and had gone to a cousin of his mother's, Sally, for Christmas Day tea, Mum was living in the village across the fields from Sally's farm and that she used to sell eggs to her. On my return to England, Sally told me she could remember Mum, as she and her family had discussed Mum's move to Canada and leaving Jenny behind. It had not been the right time for us to meet.

The most important thing I learnt however was that Mum had often thought of me and when I was wondering on my birthday or at Christmas if she was thinking of me, she had been. Mum had also kept several photographs of me, which she had been able to hide from Geoff and one was the large one sent by the NCAA, showing me standing and holding a small soft rabbit – a day I remember. Also there were photographs of Sam in his naval uniform, and when he and Mum were engaged. Once again it felt strange to be looking at photographs of the man who was my father and whom I had never met. Over the next few years, I would gather more information about her life before I was born and when I was a baby.

Mum was so much happier now knowing that somehow I had understood that she had been forced to give me up against her will for my protection, and also that the rest of the family now knew of my existence – I was no longer a secret.

It was sad saying good-bye to her, but we would write regularly and I was able to return to Canada for her 65th birthday. My brother, Chris, was also there, so after forty years I was able to spend some time again with my brother and sister, who I had never forgotten and be with Mum on her birthday.

At long last the 'pieces of the puzzle' of the circumstances of my birth and adoption were fitting into place and the final prediction the fortune-teller had told me 30 years ago had come true. But there was now still one more piece to go and that was to find my birth father and to learn more about him.

Although I thanked God for this meeting, somehow at this time all the fortune-teller's predictions coming true seemed more important.

CHAPTER 9

Alone Again

*The Lord himself goes before you and will be with you; he
will never leave you nor forsake you. Do not be afraid; do
not be discouraged.*

(Deut.31:8)

After Michael had completed his degree we decided to remain
in Cambridge and placed our Devon home on the market. Jane
moved to a local school to begin her GCSEs. Here she made
friends with the only other new girl in her class, Becky, and
because of this friendship Jane's Christian journey took a
significant turn – a journey that she later told me had begun
with her confirmation classes with Geoff Ball, and a journey
that I would become involved in, in an amazing way. She had
committed her life to Jesus the year before, but it was not until
she met Becky and her family, all committed Christians, and
attended St Barnabas Church and its youth group, that she
really grew as a Christian.

In the autumn of 1991, some eighteen months later, I
started to look for my birth father. I went into the local library
and looked for entries for a S. Miller in the phone book in the

Lyme Regis area and only found one. I now needed the courage to write to this address and see if this was indeed my father. I knew that this time I could really cause pain and upset in the lives of people who possibly did not know of my existence. But something made me continue my search and one day, when it was quiet at work, I wrote a letter asking this Mr. Miller if he had known my Mum.

A couple of weeks later I received a reply:

'Dear Mrs.Underhill, I was engaged to Penelope in 1944 and very much in love with her, when the engagement was broken off by her parents my whole world fell apart... On my first leave from Devonport I found that Penelope had married an RAF Officer, and no way could I get in contact with her...'

At the end of 1943 Sam had returned to England and during his three weeks leave he had met Mum.

'...I have tried to explain how things were during the war years, if you met someone and you fall in love with them, you spent every hour that was possible to do so in each other's company and dreading the day when you had to part. How young or old you were made no difference, but I'm afraid that the folks at home did not see it that way. Life never works out to how things you wish them to be and my parents were willing to stand-by us, they fully understood the situation. Penelope's parents thought they had the solution and did it their way. After a certain time when I knew I could not get her back I felt assured that being married to an RAF Officer and having the consent of her parents, Penelope's future could be secure. I have been married for over 40 years and have a daughter, son and three grandchildren. God Bless and keep you safe'

Now I was beginning to see the reason for my adoption from my father's side. Choices in life can cause such a rippling effect on so many people's lives, and now the 'what ifs' were creeping into my mind. But it had happened the way it had and I had been blessed in now knowing the truth and connecting once again with my birth parents.

This was the first of five letters I was to receive from Sam. When I replied to his first letter, I sent a photograph of my family and myself and said that I did not want to cause any problems with his family, but that I would like to learn a little more about him.

In the second letter Sam wrote:

'Please try to understand Wendy that the fact of you turning up into my life after so many years has been quite a shock to me, but in my heart, I am so pleased and it is only right and proper that you should have traced out your origins. I have shown your letter and photo to my wife. I did explain to her that I had been engaged to Penelope before we were married... The fact that I had told her made things a little clearer for her to understand things. I am a very lucky person to have a wife who loves me so much that no matter what turns up in our lives she will understand the situation, and help me in any way that she can."

This letter he signed 'Sam'.

From his letters I learnt that I have 'the smile and eyes of the Miller family' – no wonder Geoff had hated me. He looked forward to my letters and always ended them with 'God Bless You'. I also discovered Sam had spent his boyhood singing in the parish church choir. A retired choirmaster had taken an interest in him and offered to train him to a higher standard than the church choir master could. He once sang a duet at a public concert and the poster advertising the concert billed him as 'The Boy with the Golden Voice'.

Sam also wrote about his family – his parents, two sisters, Betty and Ann and his grandparents. Then one Saturday he rang me out of the blue. I cannot remember what we talked about but I do recall that he had a lovely Dorset accent.

In a further letter Sam wrote:

'This is certainly a funny old world, six months ago I did not really know that I would be writing to you and yet I know way back over the years there was someone trying to get in touch with me, that sounds like the spiritual world, but like ships that pass during the night everything feels different then in the daylight hours and with each letter we write I feel that all the past years are now being fulfilled, and though we have never met like the two ships there is a bond between us'.

I found great comfort in those words and I replied saying how I had often talked to him when I was a child and feeling so alone.

In December, Sam went to the Bristol Royal Infirmary to see a consultant because he was having problems with his angina. Following an x-ray, a shadow was discovered on his right lung. So at the end of January he started a course of radio-therapy for three weeks at the Royal Devon and Exeter Hospital.

Sam's last letter to me was written the following February. Katy, his daughter, who lived in Cornwall, rang me up a few weeks later to say Sam was ill in hospital and he had wanted me to know the reason why he was unable to write. Later on in March she rang me again,

"Wendy, its Katy, Sam's daughter. I know Sam would have wanted you to know straight away, but I am sorry to tell you he died today."

"Katy I am so very sorry. Thank you so much for telling me. I don't know if you want to stay in touch but you have my telephone number and address. One day I would love to meet you."

"I don't know," she replied. "Maybe, sometime later."

"Take care and thank you again for letting me know."

Knowing Sam was so ill it did not come as too much of a shock. I was saddened that we had never met, but I was grateful that I had been included in the family's grief and I did have his letters. At least we had got to know each other a little through them.

About six months later Katy wrote to me,

'*I wished that Dad could have met you, I know that's what he wished for*'.

When Katy and I finally met, I learnt a lot more about Sam.

He had joined the Navy in 1940 at the age of 16 years as a boy cadet. In 1941 he was posted to *HMS Prince of Wales* and had witnessed the sinking of the *Bismarck*. The ship had then gone on a secret mission, taking Churchill across the Atlantic to meet with President Roosevelt off the Newfoundland coast, who was on 'holiday' on his yacht. This meeting has been described as 'the most dramatic personal encounter of the War' and one at which they had begun to draft the Atlantic Charter. Although never signed, it had laid the foundations of the Allied goals for the post-war world. Sam attended the Anglo-American church parade service at which both Churchill and

Roosevelt were present and once was asked to push Roosevelt to an appointment in his wheelchair. Before Roosevelt left every sailor received a box containing an orange, two apples, 200 cigarettes and half a pound of cheese – luxuries in those days.

Later on that year the *Prince of Wales* went to the South China Seas off Malaysia to help defend Malaya from the Japanese invasion. While they were sailing down the coast of Malaya, with the *Repulse* and some destroyers, they were attacked by Japanese torpedo bombers and had to abandon the ship. *The Prince of Wales* was only nine months old and remembered as the Royal Navy's 'unluckiest ship'. Sam then escaped from Singapore and eventually made his way back to England via Ceylon [now Sri Lanka]. He was only 17 years old and when he returned to England he was immediately sent on the Russian convoys on *HMS Sultan* and then *HMS Formidable* until December 1943 when he was stationed at *HMS Drake*, Plymouth and started seeing Mum.

Ever since I had left Mum in 1949, I had been determined to find her one day and to learn more about my father and finding him still alive had been unbelievable. It never occurred to me at the time that this was all God's doing, but some years later I was to realise it had been.

In the autumn of the year Sam died, Mum came over from Canada and we were able to visit Lyme Regis for a few days. During that time she showed me the house where I had been born, and where Sam had grown up. She wanted to organise a gravestone for Weena's grave, so we visited the churchyard and found Sam's grave. It was strange standing there, on the top of the hill looking out to sea, knowing that my father was buried here. A man who I had never met, only written a few letters to and spoken to once, yet he had given me life and had been someone I had been able to talk to in my head when I was a child.

The following two years had its up and downs and then out of the blue, Michael asked me if I would like a divorce. We had gone for a short walk one cold grey Saturday afternoon in February and had hardly spoken to each other when suddenly he asked me the question.

Without a thought, I said, "Yes."

I do not know why I said 'Yes' so quickly, it just seemed the right response. Michael then went on to ask if I could support myself financially as, other than the money from the sale of the house, he would not be able to. I had a good job, now as secretary to the Librarian of the Scientific Periodicals Library, and since I knew it was the right path to take, somehow I would cope, but I was scared. I was back walking along that, dark sandy beach again, having to be strong for myself, as obviously I was no longer loved by anyone. Rejection had entered my life once more. I felt bitter and angry, especially with God.

On the plus side though it was a relief, that after all the years of feeling so unhappy at times, I would be free of wondering when the next argument would start, the days of silence between us, and always having to say 'sorry', assuming the situation must have been my fault.

We agreed not to tell anyone until Jane had finished school later that year and been accepted to read French and German at Nottingham University. It was November before we could get all three girls together to tell them what was happening. To this day I cannot recall what Michael said nor how the girls reacted, except there were a great deal of tears from them and myself. But I do know it was one of the worst things that I have ever had to face. I felt I had let my children down very badly by not trying to keep the family together. Somehow, as a child, one accepts what happens in life, even if it does take time. But as a mother, there to protect her children, however old they are, you feel unpleasant things should never happen to them. It had been difficult enough for me to know I was adopted, and now my children would have to tell people that their parents were divorced.

We then started divorce proceedings on the grounds that the marriage had irretrievably broken down because of his 'unreasonable behaviour'. Together we went through how he had treated me during our marriage, and Michael listed several incidents that I had actually forgotten. I had accepted our relationship as being 'normal' at times, when in actual fact it was not.

Michael and I decided to stay together until the divorce was absolute three months later, as he had no plans for where he was going to live or what he was going to do. At this stage I did ask him if he had ever loved me and he said, "No." He had married me because he had felt sorry for me and as he was always truthful I knew this was right.

Two days after my 50th birthday, the following January, Michael left for good. It was an emotional goodbye. We hugged each other and were both in tears – I nearly gave in and asked him to stay, but somehow I knew this was the right thing to do. Finally at the end of January the decree was made final and absolute and our marriage of 27 years had ended.

I was at my lowest ebb after Michael left. Jane was on a gap year working in Southampton and both Louise and Mary were working in Bristol. For the first time in my life I was on my own, so I took the opportunity to visit Australia as a way of celebrating my 50th birthday. It was a wonderful experience camping in the Northern Territory visiting Darwin, Alice Spring and Ayers Rock and finally Perth. It was also good for me to be amongst people I had never met before. I did not have to worry what I was saying and if I was doing the right thing. These people accepted me for who I was and if they did not like me, it did not matter.

Once I was home I had plenty of bad days and shed many tears. The 'beach' would then seem to be getting longer and lonelier. On Sundays I went to Great St Mary's, for Sung Eucharist. I would walk there, and each week I saw the spring flowers, snowdrops, wood anemones, crocus and daffodils, starting to appear along the Backs. I could see that after a long, dark, cold winter, with the promise of warmer weather, these flowers would soon be blooming, which gave me hope of better things to come and new beginnings. At this time though the flowers were more of a comfort than the church service, where I was still reciting the service from memory without giving it any thought. However, as I looked at the flowers, God was gradually creeping back into my thoughts.

In April, Jane went to Niger in West Africa, with missionaries in the Society for International Ministries (SIM)[6] for a couple of months to do secretarial work in their school for the children in Niamey. This had been planned for some time and as it was for a short time I did not worry too much, although for someone with her health problems, going to a very hot Third World country did carry a certain risk. Before she left I went with her to a service at St Barnabas Church, as they were going to have special prayers for her. Jane was asked to go to the front of the church, along with Becky's father, Andrew, who was going to lead the prayers. Andrew invited Jane's friends to come up too. For some reason I felt I had to

---

[6] See Useful Addresses.

be there too, so I went up. We all put a hand on her shoulders and Andrew started praying for Jane's mission to Niger. It was strangely moving and comforting for me to know that here were some of Jane's friends praying for her. Somehow I felt God was there with us, letting me know in particular that He would protect her and bring her home safely.

Meanwhile I had found a purchaser for the house, but really did not know where I was going to live. I was just living each day as it came, mostly in a blur. In June I decided to take a week's holiday and go back to Devon to visit friends. Once there it seemed the right thing to be amongst my old friends again, so I bought a small cottage which needed modernizing in a village not far from where I had lived before. I went back to church on a regular basis, but it was more out of a sense of 'duty' and keeping in touch with the regular churchgoers, than going to worship God.

It was around this time, when I was listening to Classic FM, that I heard an advertisement, for the Macmillan Nurses,[7] in which a man was talking about the two sets of footprints on the beach when times were good and then only one set during the difficult times when illness came and was asking "Where were you then?" It ended with "When you saw only one set of footprints it was then I carried you." This advertisement 'hit home', it seemed to be talking about the beach in my dream and how alone I felt when I was walking over the sand and leaving one set of footprints – so was I being carried? But who was carrying me? Jesus? Had He been carrying me all this time? It kept niggling away in my mind.

Now all the predictions of the fortune teller had come true I began to worry about the uncertainly of what life had in store

---

[7] See Useful Addresses.

for me, and how I was going to cope in the future. I needed to have a purpose, a meaning, for my life. I had found my birth family and now I did so much want to meet someone who would love me for who I am – just me – and not who others wanted me to be.

So I continued to avidly read my 'stars' and get long term predictions and even visited another fortune teller, but it didn't help. It wasn't enough – something was still missing in my life.

CHAPTER 10

Travels To Africa

...If you seek him, he will be found by you...
(1 Chron 28:9)

The following September, before Jane returned to Nottingham University where she was studying for a degree, she came to visit and we had a long talk about my childhood, my divorce and how all through my life I had felt so alone. That night Jane wrote in her diary:

"Had a long, deep chat with Mum this evening. I think – hope – I managed to get across more just how important my faith is to me. I found myself encouraging her not to judge Christianity on how people who claim to be Christians behave or treat others... Then we talked loads about the family and a lot about their marriage. I think it's good for me to know the reasons why it all broke down, so I can get a more realistic view of the situation and understand it more, and therefore come to terms with it more... Mum also said the one thing she really wants to know is that there's someone out there who really loves, accepts and respects her whole-heartedly for who she is. Somehow it felt too cheesy to say Jesus is that person,

so I just said the reason I'm not desperate for a bloke is because I get that unconditional love from Jesus.

Oh thank you <u>so</u> much God, that you are stability, hope and peace in all the confusions that we all put one another through... Thank you that I don't have to settle for what this world has to offer. It just makes me sad that others refuse to look beyond it. I know now more than ever that it's my job to bring the hope I know to them, in love, understanding and compassion, like Jesus and the woman at the well. It must be. Here I am, Lord, send me."

I first learnt about this passage from Jane's diary when I asked her if she could remember the conversation we had had, as I wanted to include it in this book and she read it out to me. But it was to be sometime yet and on a different continent that Jane's hopes of my learning the truth about God's unconditional love for me would actually happen. I had never been aware of anyone loving me with an unconditional love – I had had to earn love by trying to be the person others wanted me to be, so that hopefully I would then be loved by them.

So life went on and the following year was busy with a number of changes in my life, and the beginning of the wonderful, exciting steps I would be taking on my Christian journey. The year's contract for a secretarial job I had came to an end, so I decided it was time for a change and joined an agency that supplied housekeepers and carers to look after people in their own homes on a short term basis. For two years the work took me to Sussex, Somerset, Guernsey and finally to South Devon where I cared for Teresa for a couple of years.

In early summer I went on a coach tour around Scotland with my friend, Sheila and two American friends I had met on holiday in Antigua many years before, Pete and Barbara. We travelled first to the Inverness area and visited Balmoral and

Loch Ness. Sheila and I decided not to go on the boat trip around Loch Ness, as neither of us enjoyed being on boats so instead wandered round the Monastery at Drumnadrochit.

While we were in the bookshop I saw copies of a poem which seemed familiar and reminded me of the advertisement I had heard for the Macmillan Nurses; it was called *Footprints in the Sand*, by Mary Stevenson, and described a person walking on a beach with the Lord, leaving two sets of footprints behind them in the sand. At times the footprints would merge into one set when the person was going through a bad time. When questioning why the Lord was not there when He was needed most, He replied "The times when you have seen only one set of footprints is when I carried you."

Tears came into my eyes. It felt so relevant to my life. So Jesus HAD been carrying me for most of my life. I decided to send a copy of it to Jane, but did not buy one for myself – perhaps the realisation of God REALLY being there for me for all my life and the fact that He REALLY loved me and would never leave me was too new to grasp. I had spent so long feeling unloved.

Earlier in the year Jane had been planning the third year of her course in which she had to spend time in a French or German speaking country and was accepted by WEC International, on a short-term contract of nine months to work in Chad, Central Africa. For some time she had been completing a small cross-stitch picture of some flowers and when she had finished it with the words: "I have loved you with an everlasting love Jer. 31:3" she enclosed it with a letter:

'*I don't know if you remember, but we had a really long conversation about life, love and the universe, and you said how all you'd ever wanted was to be loved for exactly who you are. Well, first of all it goes without saying that I love you exactly for you, for the amazing Mum you are, but I wanted you to have a reminder of how that is the way God loves you. His love never runs out, never changes, never compromises. His love is very real and we can all know the reality of it, in fact that's all he wants and longs for. It's because of His love that I'm here and because of His love that I'm going to Chad... Because God loves me, I can trust Him, and because I trust Him I want to obey Him, and I want to be a part of His work in telling others, whether that be in Chad, in Nottingham or in my own family, of His amazing, consuming, everlasting love... I'm praying for you every day; I pray that you'll know the reality of God's love and that He'll look after you. Please pray for me too.'*

The same day that Jane wrote to me she made an entry in her diary:

'I've written to Mum explaining about how God loves her and I'm trusting it'll have a real impact. When I couldn't sleep the other night, it was like I saw and heard her saying, "Why didn't you tell me before?" I'm more and more convinced she doesn't really understand the Gospel, what Christianity is all about, and I really want to know I've done all I can in explaining the truth to her. So shall see...'

I felt worried that Jane was going to an undeveloped country again, and for a much longer time, but she told me that one of her team leaders, Louis, was a doctor and was happy to take care of her. As I learnt more about how WEC worked on the field, I realised that God would look after her and bring her home safely.

As I write this I can now see that all along God knew I would never accept Him fully into my life if He had suddenly made His presence felt in some dramatic way – He knew me too well! Instead, by using Jane's love for Him as an example and guidance, He was slowly placing thoughts into my head, letting me know He was preparing me to walk beside Him, instead of carrying me along that long, dark, sandy beach.

For many years I had wanted to visit Africa, especially to meet the Bushmen of the Kalahari. So I did some research and found a camping tour that started in Harare, Zimbabwe, went on to Botswana and finally to Namibia travelling through the Khaudom Game Reserve into Bushmanland to see the Ju/Hoansi band of Bushmen who lived on the edge of the Kalahari. The tour ended back in Harare. I wrote to Brenda's husband, John, who was now a Canon in the Anglican Cathedral in Harare to see if I could stay with him, before and after the trip.

At the end of June 1997 I set off for my long awaited trip to Africa. John met me at Harare airport and took me back to his home for breakfast. The next day was Sunday and as John was helping at the 9am Sung Eucharist service at the Cathedral he introduced me to the wife of one of the churchwardens so I could sit next to her. He had told me that there would be over 600 people attending the service, but as we started to sing the first hymn there did not appear to be many people there. There was no organist so a large choir of very enthusiastic singers led the singing. The hymns were familiar, but the words were in Shona, the local language. I did find it very uplifting singing unknown words to familiar music. Everyone was so happy rejoicing and praising Jesus, because they wanted to. When the hymn ended I quickly turned round and found the Cathedral was full and indeed during the notices people were asked to arrive on time! I thoroughly enjoyed the service and being amongst Africans who loved the Lord.

Later on that day I joined the group I was going on safari with. I found it harder this time being on my own amongst about sixteen strangers, all of whom were a lot younger than me. But I knew that if I was to see the San Bushmen joining this group was the only way I could do it. The following day we flew to Victoria Falls for two days to explore the Falls. I went on an early morning boat trip up the Zambezi, and saw my first elephants and hippopotamus. Then in the afternoon took a flight over the Falls which put them into perspective – a truly magnificent sight.

From Victoria Falls we travelled in a truck to the Chobe National Park in Botswana, which has Botswana's largest variety of wildlife. Then into Namibia along the Caprivi Strip where we met up with the three excellent guides who took us through the Khaudom Game Reserve in 4 x 4 vehicles to Bushmanland. Driving through the Reserve was unbelievable. It is crossed by a number of omuramba, fossil river valleys, which run mostly parallel to the sand dunes and they are full of reeds and grasses. The weather was warm during the day and cold at night and we stopped at designated campsites at night and waterholes for lunch. With the warmth from the sun and the only sounds coming from the odd bird singing and the gentle breeze rustling the grass, I felt as though God's arms were wrapped around me, keeping me safe. His presence was all around, but I did not know how to begin to get to really know Him, I just knew He was there. And we had to keep moving on.

After two days we left the Park and set up a bush camp for two nights near Tsumkwe, under a large and very old baobab tree. For thousands of years the San have been hunters (the men) and gatherers (the women) in the Kalahari, but in 1970 Bushmanland was established as a San homeland so they are now concentrated into a very small area which means they cannot survive using any traditional methods. Today they try to farm crops and raise cattle and goats and are gradually being absorbed into a western culture.

The following day we visited one of their villages and watched them make a fire using one stick, a difficult task, and poison for the arrows they use when hunting. We tasted some of the food the women were preparing for lunch – mealie meal – played with the children and bought items they had for sale.

In the afternoon we went to meet another group of San. Three men showed us how they set traps for animals, using sticks and string they made from the 'Mother-in-law' plant. They then acted out how they hunted steenbok and hares, with one of them representing the animal. They are wonderful actors and their enjoyment at performing was a delight to watch – there was much laughter! The women then took us on a walk to show us the different food you can gather to eat, both above and below ground. From both these two groups of San, we had a small insight into their tradition of being hunter-gatherers, moving from one place to another in the vast deserts of Southern Africa.

It had taken us six days to spend one day with the San and on our return to the truck, which would take us back to Botswana and the Okavanga Delta, I felt strangely bereft. I had finally met the San people and experienced some of their culture and now it was all over. I had also experienced the vast African bush and the extraordinary hold it can have on you. Somehow I felt part of it and I did not want to leave. But I had my memories and now a desire to return to Namibia one day

Mark, our driver and Sandy, our cook, were engaged to be married and they were both committed Christians. I spoke briefly to Sandy about this while we were travelling in the truck one day and also had a quick look at the book she was reading – *The God Who Changes Lives*[8] edited by Mark Elsdon-Dew. It was all about how various people had become Christians and the different experiences they had had. It all seemed so easy for these people – it somehow just happened to them. When and how would it happen to me? What did I have to do to make it happen? It was still a mystery to me and maybe one day it would happen, but at the moment it was not happening.

My trip had been exhausting at times with all the travelling, taking it in turns to help run the camp, and being with strangers. However I had discovered that I loved Africa and finally at the back of my mind I felt my life was beginning to take shape, that there was a challenging future ahead and perhaps this future lay in Africa in some way. Was this what God had planned for me?

I was determined to return to Africa so rang around various organisations who worked in Africa, but most of them were not interested in either someone of my age or with only secretarial qualifications. However Youth With A Mission (YWAM)[9] were very encouraging and sent me their brochure, which gave me details of the courses they ran. It was interesting, but did I really need to spend money on learning about God – surely not?

Later on in the year Jane came to spend a few days with me prior to her trip to Chad in October. By this time she knew she was going to teach English to adults at WEC's Centre de Connaissance, in a town called Abeche in the north of Chad. We had a lovely time together, but it was sad saying goodbye

---

[8] Mark Elsdon-Dew, *The God Who Changes Lives*, HTB Publication, London 1996.
[9] See Useful Addresses.

to her. I told her that if it was possible I would like to come and visit her and she promised to see if I could once she was settled, as she would also love me to come.

Jane's first Prayer Letter she sent home in December described the start of her mission in Chad. She began the letter with: 'Jeremiah 29:11 'For I know the plans I have for you', declares the Lord, 'plans to prosper you and not to harm you, plans to give you a hope and a future' – maybe God had some good plans for me? She then went on to describe Abeche, and the people she was working with. And she loved her work teaching English. I envied her writing so freely about serving God in this way. I still wanted to return to Africa to work, but did not think about it in terms of doing it for God.

Some weeks later I was able to talk to Jane on the phone and the first thing she said to me was "Mum, everything is arranged for you to visit. Can you come during the second week of January when Louis and Susan will be in N'Djamena, and then you can travel to Abeche with them? They have lots for you to do like helping in the library and doing some gardening."

I felt so happy hearing those words. Somehow I knew that this trip was going to be a turning point in my life, a step forward in my Christian journey.

CHAPTER 11

Learning More About Christianity

New beginnings are exciting – it's the faithful going on
when the excitement fades that counts.

Amy Carmichael (1867-1951)

I travelled to N'Djamena, on my 53rd birthday, arriving in the early hours of the next day. Louis and Susan, his wife, were there to meet me and we then drove through the quiet streets to WEC's guest house where we were all staying and went straight to bed. It was lovely to feel warm again after leaving a cold England, but it took some time to go to sleep as the first prayer calls were coming from the mosques and a nearby cockerel also thought it was time to wake up!

At breakfast, which started with grace – something I became used to during my stay – I got to know Louis and Susan. They were both from North Carolina and team leaders for the Abeche area. Louis was serving as medical director to a local health district, supervising and supplying ten dispensaries in various bush villages. Susan taught the top level of English at the Centre de Connaissance and facilitated language learning and orientation for new missionaries. They had been in Abeche for a year and lived at the mission station.

The following morning at breakfast I found myself telling Louis and Susan about myself, about my childhood, my dream about Jesus and how I was a Christian because I believed in God, said my prayers most days and went to church regularly. Imagine my surprise and annoyance when Susan said,

"That's churchianity nor Christianity."

"What is Christianity then?" I asked.

"Christianity," said Susan. "starts with having a loving personal relationship with Jesus, by putting Him at the centre of your life – to know Him as you would know a close friend. You need to be able to adjust your life, so that God can do through you what He wants to do."

Fine, but Louis and Susan were missionaries, so their lives were centred on this. It was all rather complicated for me to understand, especially as I knew I WAS a Christian. However it was interesting listening to them and to try to get some insight into why they and Jane had this 'glow' of happiness and contentment about them. Something I would like to have, but seemed rather difficult to achieve.

After our lengthy talk I walked round to meet the Field Leaders, Liz and Pauline, and to do some typing for them – it was good to help them in this way. In their bathroom was a large poster of a few seagulls flying against a brilliant blue sky and the words 'LET GO AND LET GOD'. I knew I had a lot to 'let go', over 50 years of my life, but 'Let God' do what? I had no idea.

Susan then joined me and we visited a nearby market so I could buy a headscarf, which I was required to wear in Abeche being a Muslim town. It was an interesting experience trying to avoid stepping on the live chickens and the raw meat for sale that was lying on boards on the ground!

The following day Louis, Susan and I set off for Abeche, the fourth largest town in Chad situated in the north 762km from N'Djamena. It was a two day hard drive in a 4 x 4 along dirt roads, which were very dusty and bumpy. Air Tchad only had one plane that flew to Abeche once a week (with the mail) on a Monday, if it was not under repair or wanted by the President.

After an overnight stop we found Jane at the mission station. It was wonderful to see her again, looking so well and happy! We hugged and hugged each other and both of us were in tears. I had arrived just at the right time. Jill, with who she shared a concession (accommodation), had been diagnosed with an aggressive cancer the week before and had had to leave within 48 hours for treatment back in the UK. Although I could not be of much help, I was someone Jane could talk to and be there for her, while she took on her extra responsibilities and adjusted to being without Jill for support. Louis then took us round to Jane's concession and more tears came to my eyes when I saw her teddy bear lying on her bed – the one I had bought for her in Bristol when she was a baby. She had made a chocolate cake for my birthday, which was a lovely surprise and it tasted very good!

The concession consisted of a long building split into three bedrooms and a kitchen. There were also two open sitting areas, another kitchen in which there was a charcoal fire, and an outside bathroom (no roof), with 'squat' long-drop loo. There was only one tap for everything, which was in the yard, but there was electricity with a few sockets. Outside the ground was sandy and there was a small flowerbed with shrubs and a tree. Within this simple and rather primitive concession was a wonderful homely atmosphere of warmth and love – no one was turned away from the door without at least a drink of water and more often than not some food.

The next day was Sunday, and after breakfast Jane and I and the other missionaries went to church mainly attended by Christians from the south of the country, who had come to Abeche to work. The church was filled up from the front, women and men on different sides, and you sat next to the last person who had sat down – that way the front rows were always filled! When the church was full, people sat outside either on benches or on mats on the ground.

As Jane and I entered the church the choir was singing a welcome song. The service then took the form of singing hymns, prayers, and readings from the Old and New Testament, all conducted in French. During the notices newcomers were introduced to the congregation. As a newcomer, Jane had handed in my name, and when it was called out I had to stand up so that everyone could see who I was. When all the names had been read, the choir sang another song of welcome. All the singing was very lively and clay pots were used as drums to add to the rhythm – rhythm being more important than melody. The sermon, in French, and lasting about 35-40 minutes long, was translated into Ngambai, the main southern language, or Arabic depending on who was there to do the translating.

After lunch and a rest Jane and I went to the Centre de Connaissance, which was just round the corner from the concession. It consisted of two classrooms and a library of school text, reference books and various journals – books and journals that school pupils would not otherwise have access to. In a cloistered area mats were laid down for people to sit on and read when the library was open during weekday afternoons. It was very quiet here and you couldn't hear any noise from the road, only the birds singing and people talking quietly. I was surprised to see sparrows and doves, and in the late afternoon swifts flying high in the sky.

So the days went by and I became used to living amongst missionaries in a small Arab town on the edge of the Sahara and to be part of the routine that Jane had established. This involved getting up early, boiling our water for everything, eating only fresh food that could be bought from the market, which was then cooked over a charcoal fire or small gas stove, talking to visitors – of which there were many – and helping Jane and Susan where I could. Lunch, the main meal of the day, was eaten about 1pm. After lunch it was time to bolt the front door and to have a rest followed by a bucket shower. Having been up since 6am and with the temperature getting higher and higher – up to 40 degrees and it was winter! – it was nice to relax and have time to yourself.

Darkness fell around 6pm and it was a lovely time of the day as you heard neighbours talking and playing their radios and the children went out onto the streets to play. The final call to prayers would then take place, dogs started barking, the cockerel gave an occasional crow, and a donkey would start braying. One night I thought an old man was snoring next door, but it turned out to be a camel that a relation had ridden on for a visit!

Bedtime was about 9pm, by which time the cockroaches appeared from the squat loo, a little disconcerting as they wandered around your legs but apparently they did a good job down in the sewers! Bed would then find me with a wet flannel on my face and a towel to mop up the perspiration – and of course my paper fan! There were no electric fans in Jane's concession and with the galvanized roof and only a little breeze at times, the bedroom remained very hot until the early hours of the morning. But best of all were the brilliant stars and bright shining moon.

One night I started to say The Lord's Prayer but to my horror I found I had forgotten all the words. It was as though I could only say the prayer if I recited it with other people. I felt very low and wondered if I would ever become a Christian and have that incredible faith that Jane and the other missionaries had. Also where did I begin?

It was not until the end of my second week in Abeche that I took an enormous step in my journey to becoming a Christian. Most Saturday afternoons the WEC team met for fellowship; a time to sing songs, study a passage from the Bible and pray for one another. For someone who had never experienced anything like this, it gave me a warm feeling being with people who shared their joys, hopes and fears with each other, knowing that God was listening to them – but would He be listening to me?

Earlier that particular Saturday I had started to feel unwell with diarrhoea, but feeling better as the day wore on, Jane and I went to the guest house for the meeting. Susan led the fellowship and after some singing, she read Psalm 84 – her favourite psalm. A discussion took place about the meaning of the psalm, which I found interesting – I had never really thought about their meaning before, just sung them to music. It was then time for everyone to share their concerns and blessings. Susan had to decide which publisher to send the book she had just finished to, and Louis was worried about how to distribute different medicines to the bush dispensaries. I was sitting between Louis and Jane. Part of me felt an 'outsider' and therefore I did not need to join in, but the other part had different ideas! Without any thought I told everyone how angry I was with all that had happened to me during my childhood and my marriage and that this anger was stopping me from reaching God. I then promptly burst into tears. Jane hugged me and we were then both crying. Everyone was wonderful and in turn prayed that I would be able to shed my anger and become closer to God.

In Jane's diary for that day she filled in some of the gaps of the meeting, parts of which I still find a blur:

'...we went to the WEC fellowship meeting and Mum made a <u>HUGE</u> step in her relationship with God, perhaps maybe <u>the</u> step. I think that what Susan shared about Psalm 84 really spoke to her, and she made some comments when we had a little time to talk about it. Then when we were giving prayer requests, she asked for prayer and burst into tears, saying she'd been a Christian all her life, and had had a vision of Jesus when she was six, but she'd been through so much hardship and though she knew Jesus had been with her in it all, she needed to get rid of all her anger, so she could "join" us. We sat there, crying and hugging, and everyone prayed for her there and then. <u>Then</u> after the rest of us had given things to pray for, she prayed out loud for Susan, which I know was a massive thing for her... I don't exactly know what is going on in the heavens tonight to do with Mum, but I pray it has catastrophic, eternal consequences for God's glory and her salvation!'

It was two days before I had recovered enough from my diarrhoea to have a long chat with Susan. In a notebook I was keeping as a record of my visit to Chad I wrote:

'Susan has made me realise I must stop being strong and let Jesus take over my anger and hurt of my childhood and marriage. She suggested that I place a Cross on the top of the hill at the end of my 'beach dream' and then I must put my hurt of being given away by Mum in one box and lay it at the foot of this Cross. Then another box for my adopted parents who could not show their love for me in the way I wanted. And a third box for my marriage with Michael – to forgive him for

the way he treated me over the years. I must realise I am not alone in this life because Jesus is always beside me. I must stop being stubborn and admit I cannot keep being strong and although I can be strong for the girls, with God's help, I must give in to Jesus' will and do what He wants me to do. I must overcome my pride because I think I can lead my life my way and not the way Jesus wants me to go. I need to shed these burdens and let Jesus take me into His open arms otherwise I will never find peace and contentment.

Susan and Jane then prayed that, with open arms, I would shed my load at the foot of the Cross. I will speak with Geoff Ball when I get home to help me. Susan and the rest of the team will also pray for me.'

In another entry I wrote:

'...must allow God to deal with my anger and give me inner peace as He is waiting to do this for me. Write down names of people I feel angry with. Kneel down by my bed and lay the paper before the Lord. Ask Him to wash my anger away from me and give me a fresh perspective on these people. Quiet reflection with God will help me to forgive and keep anger at bay.'

I also wrote down various quotes from the Bible that Susan had guided me to concerning my anger and titles of books she had recommended which would help me to learn more about being a committed Christian. In her book *Meeting God at Every Turn* Catherine Marshall writes, 'When anyone of us has a painful experience that our mind cannot equate with a loving God, there is this remedy: 'I want You and Your presence, Lord, even more than I want understanding. I choose

You'. When we ask this, He then gives peace and illumination as His gift'.[10]

In just two weeks I had started on the most incredible journey of my life. For the first time I was learning more about myself – the person God had always known about. And the most wonderful thing was that I now knew how I could become a committed Christian. Something I so badly wanted to be. But I also realised that it was easier to carry on with life the way I had become used to, rather than to step into the unknown.

---

[10] Catherine Marshall, *Meeting God at Every Turn,* Hodder & Stroughton, 1995, p508.

CHAPTER 12

I Give My Life To Jesus

*For God so loved the world that he gave his one and only
Son, that whoever believes in him shall not perish but have
eternal life.*

(John 3:16)

The first thing I did when I got home was to go to my local
Christian bookshop and buy a copy of the NIV Student Bible
and *Every Day with Jesus For New Christians*. The latter I
found to be a tremendous help in beginning my walk with
Jesus as so much of it seemed relevant to how I should be
leading my life.

One day I came across a prayer that really spoke to me:

'Lord, I do not want to go through life with bitterness and
resentment in my heart against anyone. Teach me to be a
forgiving person. In Jesus' Name. Amen'.[11]

---

[11] Selwyn Hughes, *Every Day with Jesus For New Christians*, CWR,
1994, Day 40.

It made me realise that in order to shed my burdens I had to forgive the people who had been closest to me during my childhood and marriage. I was the sinful one for carrying my hurt and anger for so long, and not being forgiving.

Then in early March I went to see Geoff and spent three hours with him pouring out my heart. Not only had Geoff taken Jane's confirmation classes, which had led her to becoming a committed Christian, but he had also given my father his last communion, so he seemed the right person to help me take that final step.

The next day I went back to the bookshop and discovered a book by Roy Lawrence called *How to Pray When Life Hurts*.[12] In the chapter 'How do you pray when life has hurt you?' Roy writes about a forgiveness prayer he came across – author unknown: 'Not all of it will apply to you, but you feel your inner self reverberate whenever a sensitive area is touched', and it certainly did for me.

That night I asked God to help me to lay my hurt and anger before Him at the foot of the Cross – I could not do it on my own. It was such a big step to take. I knew it would change my life for ever.

Then the following morning when I was reading *Every Day with Jesus For New Christians*[13] about 'assurance', I was guided to John 15: 1 – 17. As I read verse 16: "You did not choose me, but I chose you" the words leapt off the page – God had spoken to me through the words in the Bible! I promptly burst into tears. I then read on "and appointed you to

---

[12] Roy Lawrence, *How to Pray when Life Hurts*, Scripture Union, 1995. P34.

[13] Selwyn Hughes, *Every Day with Jesus for New Christians*, CWR, 1994, Day 19.

go and bear fruit – fruit that will last". I did not take in the true meaning of all the words then as I was so excited that God had spoken to me.

Suddenly I felt deep down it was now or never that I must shed my burdens. I must place the three boxes that Susan had talked about at the foot of the cross on the hill at the end of 'my beach'. So with the prayer I had read in Roy's book that I had re-written to make it personal to me and my list of burdens I needed to shed, I knelt at the side of my bed and prayed:

'Lord Jesus Christ, I ask today for your help that I may forgive everyone in my life who has hurt me. I know that you will give me strength to forgive, and I thank you that you love me more than I love myself and want my happiness more than I desire it for myself.

Lord, I truly forgive MYSELF for my sins, faults and failings.

For any delving in fortune-telling and reading horoscopes.

For taking your Name in vain. For not worshipping you.

Lord, I forgive Michael, who for 30 years I had believed loved me only to find he had married me because he was sorry for me; for putting me down at times and not allowing me to be myself and for his lack of love and affection towards me.

Geoff, for his cruelty to me and for making Mum give me away.

Mum for giving me up.

My adopted parents for not loving me how I wanted them to – by not giving me more of their time, nor being more tactile.

The friend who sexually abused me.

I am so sorry I have committed the following sins:

I cannot let go of my anger, hurt, and feeling sorry for myself.

I have this feeling of desolation of being on my own in this world – no one loves me, no one worries about me.

I am stubborn because I won't let go and let Jesus into my heart. I have to be in total charge of my life.

Not being with my adopted Father when he died and not loving my adopted Mother as I should have done.

Because of these sins I cannot find peace or contentment. I am always restless, spend too much money, relying on clairvoyants and reading my 'stars'.

Thank you, Jesus that your will is to free me from unforgiveness. Let Your will be done. Thank you for dying on the cross for me for the forgiveness of my sins and to give me eternal life.

Let your Holy Spirit fill me with light, and let every dark area of my mind be enlightened. Amen.'

When I had finished praying I saw myself walking along my 'beach' dream again. But this time I was not alone, Jesus was walking beside me and He led me to the cross on the top of the hill, at the end of the beach, and there was God standing with His arms opened wide. My 'boxes' were handed over to God – I had been able to forgive those people who had hurt me, and all my past sins had been forgiven. The cross was surrounded by a bright shining light and now I cannot see that cross without it being lit up. And one day I knew I would find the 'beach' of my dream! God was beginning to come out of His 'box'.

I could now begin a new life because the Bible told me: 'Therefore, if anyone is in Christ, he is a new creation: the old has gone, the new has come!'[14] I had also discovered what was missing from my life – I had seen Jesus in a dream, but now He was real to me.

I felt I was now being released from the past and would be able to start to discover the person God had created me to be. I knew it would take time – there would be many times when my past caught up with me, but each time I would be able to deal with it and not store it away in some dark cupboard.

Through tears of happiness and elation, I felt not only excited, but also that an enormous load had been lifted from my shoulders. I felt a different person. But I knew I still had a lot to learn about God's love for me and how He was going to use me, 'to go and bear fruit – fruit that will last'.[15] The date was 7 March 1998.

A few days later I managed to speak to Jane and tell her my news. She was so excited and I eventually received a letter from her in which she wrote:

'I can't tell you how excited I am about what you said on the phone – it's the most fantastic thing ever, and I'm so grateful to God for His goodness and faithfulness. The first passage you read in your 'Everyday with Jesus', Romans 8: 28 –39, is one of my favourites. God loves us with such a perfect love – He is huge and almighty and sovereign, but He calls us, chooses us, protects us and works for our good in such a

---

[14] 2 Corinthians 5: 17.
[15] John 16:16b.

personal and caring way. We could never, ever earn such love and approval from the Holy God by our own efforts or merits, we will never reach the standards He requires because of His perfection, on our own. That's why Jesus, who was perfect Himself, died in our place on the cross to take away our sins when we ask for His forgiveness, and bring us into a relationship with God.

It's the most amazing act of real love that this world will ever know; the son of the almighty, living God nailed to a cross, so we, each one of us, can live our lives as we were made to i.e. in a relationship with God. That's what being a Christian is, Mum – it's not about which church you go to, what label you put on yourself, how you were brought up, or how you express your faith – it's about knowing, believing and confessing that you have an on-going relationship with God, because He has forgiven your weaknesses and mistakes – the things which separated you from Him – and He let His son pay the price for them on the cross...

I'm not surprised you feel like a new person. It's like life starts over again and this time you're taking every step with Jesus. I'm also not surprised you feel free from burdens – Jesus said, 'You will know the truth, and the truth will set you free... If the son sets you free, you will be free indeed' (John 8: 32 – 36) and also 'Come to me, all you who are weary and burdened, and I will give you rest' (Matthew 11: 28).

I thank God every day for what He's done in you and all that He's given you – especially people to talk to and opportunities to grow in your faith and understanding. You must feel completely free to express your relationship with Jesus in any way that suits you – the important thing is that you have that relationship and that you get to know Him more and more, especially through reading the Bible and praying.

We need to do this individually, but God has also called us to be a church, like a family, because He knows that we need each other, for encouragement and support. So I'm praying for you, that there will be like-minded people who you can spend time with and grow closer to God with.'

Some weeks later I received a letter from Susan.

'...My heart rejoices in your news that you have found the cross on the top of the hill. What a joyous journey now lies before you. Where will the Lord lead you? What lessons will He have you to learn? Hard or joyful, the one thing to remember always is that the One who leads you does so in love. He will never fail you or forsake you...'

It was so wonderful and encouraging to read these reactions from both Jane and Susan and at long last to understand what Christianity meant – my belief in God was no longer 'churchianity'. As much as it had been so wonderful to be reunited with my Mum, moving from physical adoption to spiritual adoption would bring me eternal life. I had now discovered a very special Father who loves me unconditionally!

I had also met Jesus at the cross and could begin to have a personal relationship with Him, as I read my bible, prayed and went to church, but I still needed to learn how to adjust my life so that God could do through me what He wanted to do. I was still determined to go back to Africa one day, especially to Namibia, but this time to do God's work.

So I began knocking on various doors, one of which led me to a Christian holiday and conference centre in North Devon, Lee Abbey,[16] with a view to being part of the

[16] See Useful Addresses.

community for a year and a few weeks later I spent three days there. I was well looked after by my sponsor, Penny, and given a chance to work with the different teams and join in the worship, so I could get a feel for the place, as well as being interviewed by different people. On the first evening while I was talking to Penny I began to realise that being here would not fulfil my need to learn more about my walk with God, and to strengthen my faith in Him. Some years before Penny had completed the Crossroads Discipleship Training School (CDTS) with Youth With A Mission, which was run especially for people 35 years of age and over and for families, and the more she told me about it, the more I felt it was right for me.

The next day I was given a copy of their brochure – the same one I had received the previous year, but had put to one side – and read that the course was 'a time for spiritual renewal and an opportunity to regain insight into God's purposes for the rest of your life'. On the first page of the brochure, however, was a letter from the Director and as I read it one phase leapt off the page 'Do you hunger to know more about God and how you can effectively serve him?' Tears filled my eyes. That was exactly what I was looking for! So I filled in my application to attend a CDTS at The King's Lodge, Nuneaton, Warwickshire, and was duly accepted to join the next course the following April.

PART TWO
A TRUE IDENTITY

CHAPTER 13

Join Youth With A Mission

If you are pleased with me, teach me your ways so I may know you and continue to find favour with you...
(Exodus 33:13)

I felt very nervous stepping out into the unknown, but I knew God wanted me to be at The King's Lodge and therefore He would be at my side. Not only would this time be a time of spiritual growth – learning more about my relationship with God and His Word – but it would also be the beginning of the healing of all the scars of the past.

There were twelve of us representing four different countries and four members of staff from three different countries. Our ages ranged from late twenties to mid-fifties – me! And ten children aged from 16 months to 11 years. We were a diverse group of people, but got on very well, proving to be a great support to one another. As the weeks went by I found The King's Lodge a safe place to shed many tears.

The theme of the course was to: Equip, Challenge, Impart and Prepare, and we were given a bookmark with the words

'Here I am. Send Me',[17] the same quote Jane had written in her diary a couple of years before. Where will you send me Father? Namibia? The twelve weeks of the lecture phase went by quickly with so much to learn and absorb about God and myself. But God in his wisdom revealed different things to me a little at a time. He never left me alone and my relationship with Him became stronger and stronger. Indeed at times I felt as though I had not only been through the washing machine, but the dryer as well! The rest, I knew, would come in time with the different experiences I was sure I would encounter during outreach and subsequent years.

Every Monday morning we had 'Base Worship' and I hated it. It was so loud, and people were waving their arms around and jumping up and down! I left the first one before the end and asked a member of staff if I had to attend, but apparently it was part of the course and compulsory. As time went on I did begin to learn the songs and choruses, and eventually to enjoy many different ways of worshipping.

I found a small rural Anglican Church nearby and regularly attended their services. Maybe it was worshipping in an old church, rather than a room in a building that made a difference. I had missed listening and singing to an organ and still could not understand why drums had to be played so loudly! At one evening service in the church the theme was based on Psalm 24. People prayed and others gave their testimonies. At the end of the service there was an opportunity to go for ministry for healing. It was an awesome experience. As the lady was praying for me she said she had the word 'locusts' and I immediately remembered that I had recently

---

[17] Isaiah 6: 8.

been given the same scripture by someone else – 'I will repay you for the years the locusts have eaten'.[18]

I went home feeling very encouraged knowing that in time God, who had already restored my birth family to me, would one day give me the opportunity to experience a truly happy Christian marriage to a man of His choosing. And most of all God was restoring me to the person He had planned for me to be before I was born.

I also found intercessions difficult to begin with as I had never prayed aloud before. So many of the prayers had phrases in them that I felt I would never be able to include in my prayers and yet it seemed to be what was required as everyone said them. Then I would wonder what I would say anyway as everyone had said what had been needed to be said. It would take me a long time to have the courage to pray aloud.

I had spent 50 odd years trying to be someone I wasn't, so why was I trying to be like other Christians in the way they worshipped, prayed and spoke?

Bible study was also a struggle at times, trying to understand everything I was reading and to find where all the different books were. But gradually I began to find my way around and to underline the relevant quotes, especially those that meant something to me. So the Bible provided me with guidance on how I should live my life, where to go, what to do and how to relate to others. I discovered it was full of encouraging words, along with God's promises for my life, which He would never break. It is literally my 'bible' for everyday living, giving me a purpose for my life and fulfilment.

---

[18] Joel 2: 25.

I was amazed when I remembered that I had decided not to take Religious Education at GCE, because I thought I might find that God was not who I believed Him to be. Now I was beginning to learn who God is and would always be, and it was so exciting!

Early on in the course we learnt about hearing God's voice and was directed to ask Him "What do you think of me/how do you see me?" and "What do you think I should do in the future?" When I asked God what He thought of me the only response was how I saw myself – bossy, impulsive, grumbled too much, had too many negative thoughts and needed constant reassurance from God that He loved me. It was so hard to get it into my head that God had and would always love me and it was others who had let me down and rejected me. So I left that question for another time.

When I asked Him about the future it was a shock. I was imagining the African bush, but nowhere in particular, when suddenly I shouted out the word 'Mozambique'! Why Mozambique when I wanted to go back to Namibia? It was on the other side of Africa.

When finally the answer came to what God thought of me, He told me I was, "A bruised reed He will not break".[19] Such comforting and loving words as I knew then that God would continue restoring me from all that had happened in my past and to use me to help others who have been through similar experiences.

The most revealing week was called the 'Character of God', which included how, when you hear God's voice and act, He can do amazing things for people. Randy Thomas, our lecturer, came from a YWAM base in America. With his great

---

[19] Isaiah 42: 3 and Matthew 12:20.

sense of humour he brought the Bible alive, especially when he illustrated his talks with interesting stories of how God had worked in different people's lives.

Randy began one of his lectures by telling us the story of how he and his wife had adopted a Japanese baby four years before. I was immediately interested in seeing adoption from the adoptive parents point of view rather than from my own. It was an incredible and enthralling story and he ended by describing the court scene when the final adoption papers were signed by the judge. Before the judge signed the papers, he stated that the mother had to relinquish all rights to her child because Randy and his wife would be shown as the birth parents on the birth certificate. When the mother said she did, Randy banged his fist on the desk, as the judge would have done, and for the first time I realised what a sacrifice my Mum had made in giving me up.

The next thing I knew I was calling out, "Please God forgive me," and promptly burst into tears. I had never understood before how awful it must have been for Mum. All I had wanted to do was to find her and learn why she had had to give me up.

After the coffee break I went into the grounds as I needed to be on my own to think things through. I found a trunk of a tree to sit on and as I waited on God I began to see, in some very small way, the anguish He must have felt when He watched His only son, Jesus, being crucified for the atonement of all our sins, because there was no other way. And so a little too of how Mum must have suffered when she said goodbye to me believing she would never see me again – 'a death' but knowing I could still be alive somewhere.

In one of the letters I received from Mum soon after we met again, she wrote:

'Shortly before my fifth birthday I started going to a school which was run by Anglican nuns, who were the ones mainly instrumental in turning me into an agnostic. They were so rampantly anti-Roman Catholic, and brain-washed us so thoroughly, that when my Roman Catholic step-sister insisted on showing me around her church, when I was 14, I was terrified and thought I'd probably be zapped by a thunderbolt for daring in go in there. It seems ridiculous now, but I was a remarkably innocent person at that time.'

I was so excited about all the things that God was doing in my life that I felt I had to share some of them with Mum in the hope that she would be able to understand some of it and want to ask questions. So I told her:

'...how very special you are to me because you made that sacrifice to give me a better life. Without you and Jane I would not be here today doing this course and discovering such wonderful things about God's love for me. Several people here have told me that they feel the best years are yet to come for me which makes me feel very excited! I wish you could feel this way too, because I know how hard it has been for you over all these years, and to know that you are truly happy, and at peace by knowing Jesus loves you and wants to heal you of all your past hurts as He is healing me'

When Mum replied that 'she wasn't angry for herself, but for the people she loved', I responded by sending her the forgiveness prayer I had said when I gave my life to Jesus hoping it would mean something to her too. I would hate for her to die without finding happiness in her life through the knowledge that Jesus died, so that not only could she have eternal life, but to understand about forgiveness and what a wonderful release it is when we forgive and are forgiven. All I can do now is pray for her.

The lecture phase ended on an excellent week with Paul Bennison talking on 'Goals, Dreams and Visions' – a time to relax and listen to some wonderful stories of God's power whilst being given inspiration to go and achieve whatever He wanted us to do at whatever the cost.

My final interview with the course leaders went well. I was told I had changed so much, but I did not feel that different except I knew my priorities had changed. I would now be leading a God centred life. And for the first time in my life I felt accepted for the person God created me to be and I could experience that wonderful unconditional love that only God could give me. I had found my true identity. All the fears and worry about the future were beginning to recede and although I had no idea what I would be doing in Mozambique, I knew with God, I could do anything! But before then I was returning to Harare for our seven week outreach – and this time as a committed Christian!

Towards the end of the course the girls told me that their father was getting married in September and moving to New Zealand where his new wife came from. They seemed happy about it for which I was thankful. As for me I was happy I had my 'dreams, visions and goals' to go where God wanted me to go. Two years before I would have felt very bitter, but thankfully my life was very different now.

CHAPTER 14

Missionary Work In Southern Africa

My grace is sufficient for you, for my power is made perfect in weakness.

(2 Cor. 12:9)

What was it about Africa that had such a hold on me? Was it the people, the culture, the brilliant blue skies, the wonderful sunsets, the dramatic storms or looking for the Southern Cross and Milky Way amongst the millions of stars? I believe God was giving me all these desires so that I could cope with all the possible hardships and experience all the blessings that were ahead of me.

Our first ministry was working with an Apostolic Faith Mission (AFM) church in a village in the bush called Nyamweda. Everyone was very friendly and welcoming. The families stayed with other families and all the single ladies slept on the floor of the church. There was electricity, but no running water and a pit latrine at the bottom of the compound. Washing took place behind a bamboo screen and I managed to take a couple of 'African style showers', but was very grateful that I had remembered to bring plenty of wet wipes!

The services were wonderful. Everyone was so passionate for Jesus and after every song people were calling out 'Amens' and 'Alleluias'. When the services began everyone clapped and sang in English "When Jesus says 'Yes' no one can say 'No'!" Praying was done individually aloud. Then there would be a message and finally people went up for ministry and healing. I never dreamt that I could so easily join in all the singing and dancing and enjoy it so much.

I was asked to give a talk to the Ladies Group. After praying I decided to talk about 'Adoption' – my journey from physical adoption to spiritual adoption and chose for my text: 'For He chose us in Him before the creation of the world to be holy and blameless in His sight. In love He predestined us to be adopted as His sons through Jesus Christ in accordance with His pleasure and will'.[20]

I told the ladies about the hurt, anger, abuse and rejection I had gone through during my life, and how I had slowly come to realise that God had never abandoned me. I also told them about my conversion and how I was discovering my true identity in God and how much He loves me and wants the best for me. The talk went well and was helped by an interpreter so that I had time to see from my notes what I was going to say next!

Jane had her graduation from Nottingham while I was here and as it was the first time that I had not been around to share in a special occasion with any of my children, I found the day a struggle. I was finding it so difficult at times to give my children over to God, but I knew I had to do this if I was to be an effective missionary. I had to trust God to take care of them. God had given me three beautiful girls as a gift for a specific

---

[20] Ephesians 1: 4-6.

time in their lives and now I must hand them back and let Him guide and protect them.

The whole experience at Nyamweda had been something I would never forget. It had been a very special time sharing my faith with other Christians from a totally different culture, but in Jesus we are all 'as one'.

A small group of us went to another village in the bush for three days some time later, with members of Harvest Christian Fellowship, to help with their discipleship amongst the Christians in the local villages. We held a service in the home of the family where we were staying and many people including lots of children attended. We sang worship songs, prayed and gave testimonies and afterwards several people came for healing and others to accept Jesus into their hearts and lives.

During our time there we prayed daily for a lady who had become blind following a brain tumour. Sometime later I learnt that she had not only regained her sight, but also became a Christian and subsequently started a cell church, one of the members being the local woman witch doctor!

We also had opportunities to spend time in two orphanages and another time I helped feed some of the homeless in Harare – a scheme run for many years by the Anglican Cathedral.

Having thought I had done my share of preaching I was then asked to give a talk at a local Presbyterian Church during their evening service – a very daunting prospect as the congregation was rather large and there would be no need for an interpreter. Once again I chose the topic of 'Adoption', but expanded it to the extent that my talk lasted for 50 minutes and the service ran over by 30 minutes. The Minister's comment at the end was "I didn't know Anglicans could talk for so long!"

Towards the end of our stay a few of us travelled by overnight train to Mutare, on the Mozambique border, for a Prayer Walk. Mutare, being a garrison town, had many problems with street kids, prostitution, border hopping and the highest incidences of Aids in Zimbabwe at that time.

On our arrival we went directly to the Holiday Inn for breakfast and to discuss where we should go and decided on Cross Kopje, a small hill with a cross on the top, which overlooked both Mutare and Mozambique. When we reached the top we sang worship songs, read the bible and prayed for Mutare and Mozambique. I was reminded of Moses sending the spies into Canaan and on their return saying 'We went into the land to which you sent us, and it does flow with milk and honey!'[21] At that time I had no idea why God had given me this verse and why the connection with Mozambique. It had been good seeing the country from a distance, but now I was even more apprehensive about going there on my own.

We had been warned by the taxi driver who took us to the Kopje to be aware that it was a 'border jumping' place and people had been killed there. None of us were deterred by this, but as we were leaving we met a young man coming up the hill carrying a bible in one hand and a baseball bat in the other!

We also had times to relax and to see more of this beautiful country. I was able to visit the Kariba Dam, spend a day at a local game park and travel to the YWAM base in Bulawayo, to attend their National Conference. Three of the staff celebrated their birthdays while we were here so we all went out for a meal and it turned out to be the same restaurant

---

[21] Numbers 13: 27.

where I had eaten on my final evening of the safari I had been on exactly two years before! Never in my wildest imagination had I thought I would be back there again and with a group of missionaries. I really do believe that God has a sense of humour!

There were difficult times during these weeks of outreach, especially having to cope with the constant demands of doing something out of my 'comfort zone'. As much as I was enjoying the course it would be good to complete it now and have time to assess my own personal relationship with God.

Looking back on my CTDS it had been an incredible experience and one that not many people of my age find themselves doing. In a few short weeks I had learnt so much about God, how He featured in my life, and now would always be part of my life. I had learnt my way around the Bible, been able to deliver a sermon, pray out loud, and made lots of new friends – friendships that would last.

I now had to put my mind to making plans to go to Mozambique. I had no doubts that this was where God wanted me to go and having a stubborn streak also helped me to stay focused, especially when family and friends were trying to be helpful and suggested I did other things.

John Henry Newman once said 'God has created me to do Him some definite service. He has committed some work to me which he has not committed to another. I have my mission. I am a link in a chain, a bond of connection between persons. He has not created me for nothing. Therefore, I will trust him. He does nothing in vain. He knows what he is doing'.[22]

---

[22] Source not known.

After several emails and telephone calls it was arranged that I would go to the YWAM base in Beira where a 'street kids' project was running and from there decide what I could do. So I booked a flight to Harare for late October. There was no turning back now.

The next few weeks were busy tying up loose ends and saying 'goodbyes' to family and friends. The flight, via Nairobi, went well and I had wonderful views of Mts. Kenya and Kilimanjaro and a spectacular sunrise. I spent two weeks in Harare staying with friends and helping in the office at the YWAM base. During this time though I learnt that the Beira base was being handed over to the national missionaries and all the international people were leaving. This was very unsettling as I now definitely had no idea what I should do. I knew God had called me to Mozambique, but where and for how long? Perhaps now was the time to seriously think about applying to go to South Africa the following April to do the YWAM Primary Health Care Course. My heart and desires were still strongly leading me back to Namibia and to do this course would give me a ministry to help the Bushmen.

Mozambique was still recovering from 17 years of civil war which had ended in 1992 and one soon became aware of it being very poor, with little education and medical facilities, making life a struggle for most people. However there were signs of development with a BP petrol station and a Shop Rite Supermarket recently opening in Beira.

I spent two weeks in Beira and it was a culture shock. As I wrote in my diary

'I don't mind stepping out of my comfort zone, but not to the extent of have to share one shower with loo, with loads of teenage boys, using buckets of water from a tap down two flights of stairs!'

I was also finding it difficult to know what God really wanted me to do and why I was here. Once again I wrote in my diary:

'God do you really want me here? Please help me and show me where You want me to be. I feel such a new and immature Christian. What are you teaching me Lord? Trust and patience?'

Within a couple of weeks God opened the door for me to go to work at Maforga Mission about 100kms from Mutare. The Mission had started in 1985 by Roy and Trish Perkins as a need for the many children that were made homeless during the civil war. At one time there had been 250 children, but now there were about 150, with babies and young children being encouraged to stay with their extended family. There was also a clinic, a primary school, a farm for growing crops, and batik and pottery workshops. A gift shop on the main road sold the crafts, as well as soft drinks, crisps and sweets. Finally there was a church, where the services were mainly in Shona and Portuguese, with translation into English for the sermon.

About twelve single people and seven families were working at Maforga, mostly from the UK, together with many local people. We mainly ate western food and the cook, who was new, was willing to learn western recipes, although one day we had an 'upside down' shepherd's pie! Maforga also had links with home as items of clothing were received through Operation Sunshine which friends at home were involved in. In fact I saw a boy wearing a sweatshirt from a local prep school!

After a few days I started to get to know some of the other missionaries and my work duties were sorted out. The clinic mainly served children and young adults living in the area because of the lack and availability of medication, and much to my delight I was able to spend the mornings there observing and helping where I could. The nursing sister in charge, Joan, known as Nana, was helped by Josephine from Zimbabwe and three local women who gave injections, and dressed wounds. Nana was happy to teach me about the different illnesses and diseases that affected the local people and taught me how to use a stethoscope so I could hear the difference between pneumonia and bronchitis.

I also fetched drugs from the store and counted out tablets to give to the patients. Sometimes I made temporary 'splints' for fractured arms, arranged transport to get those needing more treatment to hospital, and occasionally doing this myself. Many of the patients were young babies suffering from malaria and all the different conditions that are associated with it. There were also cases of diarrhoea, worms, chest and ear infections and a variety of rashes, as well as burns, snake bites, abscesses, STDs, and the symptoms of HIV.

From Monday to Friday we started work at 8am and sometimes did not stop until 1pm. On an average 70 patients were treated each day and occasionally it rose to over a 100. Although I was not able to be much help I was able to learn a great deal about the way the local people lived and tried to cope in difficult circumstances.

For a couple of months another missionary and I went to stay in the house of a couple who were on leave to help look after the orphan boys. They lived on a compound about a mile away from Maforga called Chegueda. The boys mostly looked after themselves, but the younger ones, about 20 of them, were given a snack at tea-time which I organised. I was also there if any of them were sick, mostly with malaria and tummy aches brought on by eating unripe mangoes! The electricity was continually going off and we only had water when the electricity was on. The nearest telephone was in the next town. Being the rainy season I soon discovered the roof of the house leaked and as time went by I found myself moving my bed around the room until I eventually found an area which was dry!

I also learnt to cope with the knowledge that this part of Mozambique had the highest population of snakes, many being so poisonous they could kill you in minutes. At that time there was very little anti-venom available. One afternoon, when I was watching some of the missionaries playing volley ball with the boys, a boomslang fell out of a mango tree. Within seconds the boys were throwing stones and it was soon killed. One of the stones must have hit the snake's stomach as three undigested baby birds fell out and were immediately eaten by one of the dogs!

Christmas was also very different from anything I had ever experienced before. I soon discovered that it is often a good idea to volunteer first when there is a list of tasks to be done which meant that I found myself decorating the church, while others butchered three-quarters of a cow, which had four legs and two tails, and others plucked and prepared forty chickens!

Following the church service the staff 'served' about 200 adults and children with sudsa, rice, and beef or chicken stew which had been cooked by some of the local woman. Then later on in the afternoon the children opened their presents which the mission had bought for them. It was a very humbling experience as I watched one of the small boys aged about eight years discover a red plastic plate he had been given. He felt it all over with one of his hands not believing it was brand new and was his to keep.

I eventually got home to open the best Christmas present I have ever had which was a packet of Maltesers sent by Sarah! I also received a card from my friend Hilary, who told me she had been praying for the last thirty years for me to become a committed Christian.

At the start of the New Year I was able to spend time with Pastor Emmanuel. He came from Zambia, pastored a local community and lived at Maforga. He believed that if I was to work in Africa I needed to learn about African culture to have a better understanding of how difficult it was for so many Africans to let go of their ancestral spirits, demons and witchcraft when they become committed Christians. I soon realised after our first meeting that he had such a lot to teach me, especially concerning my relationship with God.

One Sunday in church Emmanuel prayed, that in order to have a heart relationship with God, we all need to climb the mountain to see the 'land of milk and honey'. Suddenly the words God had given me on Cross Kope in Mutare made sense. It was not the land of Mozambique flowing with milk and honey, but my relationship with God. During one of our meetings, while Emmanuel was praying, he felt God say that He had a special job for me to do. I wrote this down at the back of my bible and thought nothing more about it until I read it several years later and realised these words had come true!

Although I enjoyed helping out at the clinic, and being with the boys, it was very much a 'desert time', as I felt very cut off from anything I was familiar with. I missed my family and friends so much at times. Josephine told me she called Maforga the 'diamond cutting factory' as she had seen so many people coming here to be shaped by God to do bigger things.

I left Maforga the following March with mixed feelings. There had been times of loneliness and internal struggles as God showed me where I needed to change, but I had also learnt a tremendous amount in a short time about Africa and its people. Now it was time to go to Worcester in South Africa to begin another YWAM course, this time on the Introduction to Primary Healthcare.

CHAPTER 15

More Training With Youth With A Mission

Whatever you have learned or received or heard from me,
or seen in me – put it into practice. And the God of peace
will be with you.

(Phil.4:9)

The YWAM base in Worcester is situated on the outskirts of the town, and at one time had been a hospital. There were only five of us on the course, Rebecca from South Africa who I shared a room with, Kathy from also from South Africa in Piketiberg, Kylie from Australia, who I had already met in Harare, and Connie from America. There were three staff members, Kim our course leader, Rene, and Trish from England. As Trish and I were the only two on the base from England we soon became life-long friends. The bible verse I was given for this course was: 'Know that the Lord has set apart the godly for himself; the Lord will hear when I call to him'.[23] I felt this was very encouraging and a good beginning.

---

[23] Psalm 4: 3.

Also on the base was Linda, a South African, who was only a couple of years younger than me, and was working in the office before starting her DTS. She became a good friend and helped to make any difficult times more enjoyable. As Linda had a car we would often drive into town for coffee and cake and also visit local tourist attractions. One weekend I went with her to her home town of Oudtshoorn, in the Little Karoo, to meet her family.

The twelve weeks of the course proved to be exhausting and challenging at times, but also very satisfying as I achieved things I never thought possible. The day began at 5.15am when Rebecca and I cooked the porridge for breakfast. This was our daily 'work duty' which left us free during the late afternoon while others were doing theirs. We then had lectures for most of the day on anatomy, physiology, midwifery, child development, prevention of most common diseases, discovering all God's health laws in Leviticus, how to work in a community, preparing healthcare lessons to give on outreach, a project on HIV/AIDS and complete a Red Cross First Aid Course. Every Monday evening we had a test on the previous week's work, something I always dreaded, but somehow managed to do well in.

On Sundays I attended the United Reform Church which was one of the few English speaking churches in the town and became a regular member. I felt comfortable with the format of the service and enjoyed the worship, joining the choir for special events.

However, as the course progressed I found it more and more difficult coping with living in a community. I was beginning to feel homesick, missing my children and family, and at times felt almost claustrophobic not being able to go for long walks across Dartmoor or along the South-West Coastal

Footpath. I needed these wide open spaces to worship God, not in a hall surrounded by others, and also silence for praying. Finding opportunities for 'quiet times' could be difficult, so I developed the habit of talking to God at any time of the day and this helped a great deal.

Outreach was finally revealed and I was going to return to Mozambique for four weeks, the last place I really wanted to go back to. This time though we would be staying on the YWAM base at Dondo, which is between Beira and Maforga. As they ran courses on primary health care, they had plenty of contacts with the local hospital and clinics. On our way back to Worcester we would travel to Emanguzi in Kwa-Zulu Natal, not far from the Mozambique border, where we would spend two weeks attached to a local hospital. We would be travelling overland by bus and train, a total of 2,500 miles!

As the lecture phase came to an end and final preparations for outreach were completed, a door began to open for me to go to Namibia. Following a conversation with one of the students on the base, Danie, I discovered he had a friend who was working with a church in Namibia who ministered to the Bushmen. He would try and obtain more details while I was away. I left for Mozambique with great expectations that finally God was granting me the desires of my heart.

Our long journey to Mozambique began by catching the overnight train from Worcester Station to Johannesburg , then by coach to Harare where we stayed overnight in the YWAM guest house. Then the following evening we took the train to Mutare where we found taxis to the border, and then a Zimbabwean, who had an empty jeep, was travelling to Chamoio where we could catch a local bus, called a 'chappa'. God, as He had done for me on my previous visit, faithfully provided us with the means of help across the border and transport to our destination.

We arrived in Dondo early in the afternoon to be welcomed by two DTS students who I had met before in Beira. It was also strange to realise that less than a year ago I had visited the base for a quick visit not knowing or even imagining I would be returning for four weeks – God is certainly full of surprises and I am glad I don't know too far in advance where He is going to lead me otherwise I know at times I would have great difficulty in being obedient.

Our accommodation consisted of two rooms, plus a wash room for bucket showers and a sit down loo without a flush. We slept on mats on the floor under mossie nets. All our water had to be collected in buckets from a well and then boiled and on two occasions I lost the bucket down the well! We cooked our meals on a two ring gas cooker. It was very much like living in Chad again and throughout my time in Africa I was always grateful for the grace God gave me to cope with things I would normally hate or evade – 'if only my friends could see me now'!

We quickly established a routine of rising early for 'quiet time' before breakfast, and then most days getting ready to go to the local hospital or a nearby clinic situated at a sugar factory, to teach, observe and complete a number of practical procedures we were being tested on, ranging from taking blood pressures and temperatures, wound care, weighing babies and patient interviews and examinations. We also had to prepare lessons which were either taught at the hospital, bush clinics or a local school which I thoroughly enjoyed. Each lesson was translated twice, from English to Portuguese and then the local language.

One Sunday I preached in a Baptist church in a small village near Dondo. The church was not very big with benches for men to sit on one side and women on the other and a lectern which was almost too high for me to read from! We had a time of worship, dancing, prayers, reading of Psalms and an offering. It was then my turn to give my message on 'Encouragement' which I based on Paul's letter to the church at Thessalonica where he tells them 'To encourage one another and build each other up'.[24]

During my talk I got everyone to walk around the church telling each other how much Jesus loves them. There was such joy on their faces as they smiled and laughed with one another. Once again the message had to be translated twice, and at times was difficult as I was never quite sure when the second translator had finished!

The leaders on the base were involved in a prison ministry, so one afternoon we were taken to the local prison to join in their worship and take some medicines. This was an experience I would never forget. About 100 men and 5 women were awaiting trial for various crimes from murder and rape to stealing a loaf of bread. The conditions were far removed from our British prisons with single story buildings around an open courtyard where there was only one tap for water, which seemed to be permanently running. The prisoners slept in the buildings on the concrete floor and it was very overcrowded. There was a bathroom of sorts attached to the rooms. When they arrived the prisoners would only have the clothes they stood up in and would have to rely on relatives or friends to bring more clothing and blankets. They were given porridge twice a day to eat. As we stepped into the courtyard, from one of the rooms, came the sound of a group of men worshipping

---

[24] 1 Thessalonians 5: 11.

and praising God. For a short time, once a week, they were able to forget where they were and look beyond their circumstances, knowing that God loved them and would never forsake them and this showed on their faces as they sang. It was strange to think that if they had not been sent to prison they may never have known Jesus.

That night I could not get the image of the prison out of my head and while I was trying to get to sleep, I recalled an incident in my childhood. I was looking out of the window at the stars and had done exactly the same thing when I couldn't get to sleep at my first boarding school. I had always thought I was just questioning God about why the different things had happened to me as a child and why my birth father had 'died', but now I realised I had been angry with God, accusing Him of my situation and with that I began to cry. So I asked God for His forgiveness for believing I was not loved, not valued by Him. Peace then set in. Gradually all the hurts of my childhood were being healed and the memories becoming easier to bear.

The following morning during Devotions, I spoke on: 'He tends his flock like a shepherd; he gathers the lambs in his arms and carries them close to his heart; he gently leads those that have young'.[25] Kim told the story of the shepherds in Israel breaking a lamb's leg if it kept straying and then carrying it around their neck until the leg was mended. This way the lamb would never stray again because it could not do without the shepherd. On hearing that story I felt very much that God had 'broken my leg', as I knew without a doubt I could now never live my life without Him.

---

[25] Isaiah 40: 11.

When I needed to get away from everyone and have some space, I would take a chair and sit under a mango tree and fill my diary with all my frustrations. One day I wrote:

'In our Devotions time today Kim talked about Isaiah's commission and how God had brought Isaiah to a time when he was broken, was then able to ask God for forgiveness, be cleansed and finally sent forth by God – 'Here am I. Send me![26] *Father, it has been such a hard time. Every time I think I am ready, that there is nothing else that needs to be sorted out, you are off again convicting me of something else! Sometimes it is such a struggle and my stubbornness won't go away! Why am I so frightened of completely submitting myself to you? I know it is the right and only thing to do, but it seems as if I should lose my identity. According to others Father, you are changing me a great deal but I don't always see it. What am I to do to be in that position that Isaiah was in before you commissioned him? I know you want to send me Father when the time is right and it seems to be taking for ever at the moment!*

At times I would become frustrated and disgruntled with the others when no one had been to the well to refill the buckets or tidied up our room. I would then wear my martyr's hat, grumbling under my breath, when I fetched and carried ten buckets of water from the well one day in order to fill up all the containers and then six the following day. My entire fault as I would expect people to do what I would do and they never did!

Finally our time in Mozambique came to an end. With Kim having only stayed for a week, Trish already flown home suffering from malaria and Rene going to her parents once we

---

[26] Isaiah 6: 8.

reached Johannesburg as she was also sick, there was only the four of us now going on to the next stage of our outreach to Emanguizi.

Once again God showed His faithfulness in our journey back to Harare. A new coach, with plenty of room, stopped outside the base, and then when we arrived at Chamoio a taxi was waiting to leave for the border. It was a quiet, hot, Sunday afternoon when we reached the bus stop at the border and there were only two cars parked in the lay-by – one man wanting to change currency which was very common and the other was a taxi. Not only was the taxi driver willing to take us right through to Mutare, (it was unusual for a taxi driver to have a passport) but it was an old car and could fit all five of us and our luggage. To this day I believe him to be an angel, as although he offered to take us to the railway station later in the evening, we never saw him again! Only God could have sent that taxi for our use.

We had a few days rest in Harare where I stayed with friends from my CDTS before our journey to Emanguzi – a long trip with another night spent travelling in a bus. I thoroughly enjoyed my time here going round the children's wards, attended out-patients, and going out with one of the mobile clinics to villages far from town. Whereas malaria and diarrhoea were prevalent in Mozambique, here it was TB, HIV and hypertension. We attended a local Evangelical church, with lots of worship, but more gospel music than I had experienced in Zimbabwe and Mozambique and once again were made very welcome.

Although hard at times, both the lecture phase and the outreach had been a time of confirming where my heart lay, in helping people, through healthcare, living in rural areas in Namibia. In the meantime I had a week's holiday before starting another three month course on Foundations in Community Development and then going home for Christmas.

Through the church I attended I met the Carter family, Brian and Cheryl, and their three children, who offered me accommodation while I did the course. It would be good to be in a family environment again and to have a bedroom all to myself!

CHAPTER 16

Home On Sick Leave

But I will restore you to health and heal your wounds,
declares the Lord.

(Jer.30:17a)

It was not long before I realised that I had made a mistake in doing this course – it was not what I had expected and so after four weeks I decided to leave. The previous nine months had been very demanding and I was now feeling spiritually, emotionally and physically exhausted.

So the following weeks before I flew home for Christmas were then spent being involved in different church activities and a wonderful unexpected visit to Namibia. Since I had come back from outreach I had been in touch with Pastor Dawie Le Roux, Danie's friend, who was working with an Apostolic Faith Mission Church (AFM) in the north of the country, in a town called Grootfontein, teaching Bushmen who wanted to become pastors. Dawie was interested in my healthcare training and now I had some free time it was agreed that I fly to Namibia to meet him and the Pastor of the church,

Boet Prinsloo. I was so excited – at long last something positive seemed to be happening!

Grootfontein lies on the road from Windhoek to the Caprivi Strip in the north-eastern part of Namibia and with Tsumeb is part of the Otavi triangle being the main region for producing maize. Grootfontein is Afrikaans for 'Big Spring'. It is a very green town and in the spring, the time I was visiting, the many Jacaranda trees in their magnificent purple were coming into bloom.

I stayed with Carl and Ruth, from Canada, who were also working with the Bushmen in Bushmanland and during this particular week Carl was there, so Ruth and I went to join him for a night. I visited several clans where Carl led services and found my desire to work with the Bushmen was still very strong. It was a productive week as I was accepted by Pastor Boet to work under the church's umbrella taking preventative healthcare to the Bushmen.

The time came quickly for me to fly back to England for Christmas with my family – and to see some snow! Then it was back to Worcester while I waited to hear about my work permit for Namibia. My extended South African visa was about to expire when I heard that I could go to Namibia on a three month's visitors' visa while I waited for a work permit. So in mid-May I said 'good bye' to all the very good friends I had made during my year's stay in Worcester and with Cheryl set off to drive to Grootfontein, the idea being to camp and visit various scenic places on the way.

However, as I kept on discovering for the next two years, life is never quite how you plan it! The day we reached Namibia my Land Rover broke down about two miles from the border – both the gearbox and the clutch had worn out. So instead of visiting the Fish River Canyon and other places,

Cheryl and I found ourselves squashed in a tow truck being driven the 800kms to Windhoek. During this fifteen hour trip we had a blow-out on one of the rear tyres of the tow truck and ran out of petrol 20kms from the nearest town when it was dark. It was very obvious that God had sent plenty of angels to look after us as we came to no harm!

I was able to stay with a friend I had met on my previous visit while I waited for six weeks to have the Land Rover repaired, to sell it as it was no longer considered reliable, and to buy another 4 x 4. I then drove to Grootfontein to start settling into my new home, which was in a flat on a farm about two miles outside of town. Being above the guest rooms it was light and airy and had great views of the bush and mountains.

I now only had another six weeks left on my visa and still no confirmation of my work permit, so I had to arrange another visit home and as I was not allowed to work I spent this time getting to know Boet and Magda his wife, Dawie, Dawie's wife, Trudie, Linda who was working with AIM, and other members of the church. I also started to learn Afrikaans with Dawie's help, something I was never able to fully grasp and instead found myself helping others to improve their English!

Going home brought yet another change to my plans as my four week trip turned into an eleven month stay. I had been feeling very tired, losing weight, my hands were shaking and my blood pressure was very high and I had put this down to the heat and adjusting to living in another country and culture. However following blood tests I found I had Graves Disease – an over-active thyroid – and that it was going to need long term treatment. I was completely thrown by this news and could not understand why this was happening. Had I been rushing ahead and not waiting to hear from God? Was I making my own agenda and trying to 'out-run' God?

At this time though all I could think about was that I had made a complete mess of my life – no home to go back to, possibly no future in Namibia and I hated having to rely on others for a roof over my head. But deep down I knew I had to hang in there and trust God for all my needs and for good times ahead. I also needed to remember that God was in control of my life and that my relationship with Him was the most important thing, not my ministry. In the meantime I would use this time to deepen my relationship with Him and to wait on His timing.

As I sought God I could see that my desire to work amongst the Bushmen was making me stubborn and prideful and the more things went wrong the more stubborn I became. I was not listening to God, only to what I wanted. God had gently closed the door on Namibia and the Bushmen until I was ready physically and spiritually to return in His timing. I had to 'let go and let God' and give all my desires to work in Namibia and with the Bushmen back to God

So I spent the following eleven months staying in my old cottage in Devon, which Louise now owned, visiting friends and family, as well as spending a couple of months back at The King's Lodge. At times I found resting very difficult to do, and on one occasion emailed a couple of friends, Susanna and Carol. Susanna replied saying that she had been praying with one of her prayer partners who felt the Lord was saying, "REST", not yet!" She also felt that:

'You need to spend time soaking in His presence and He would show you 'when'. He is preparing you for the next level and that is why the sickness has gone out of control. You are not the only disciple He is using ill health to enforce rest in

order to allow that person time in His presence. He just wants you to rest in Him and not be impatient, or strive, but be surrendered in Him. "Nestle NOT wrestle. As God said to Isaiah 'Even youths grow tired and weary, and young men stumble and fall; but those who hope in the Lord will renew their strength. They will soar on wings like eagles; they will run and not grow weary, they will walk and not be faint'." (Isa.40: 30-31)

Carol responded with a wonderful version of Psalm 23:

'My beloved one, I am your Shepherd, you will not want for anything. I am making you lie down in green pasture. So often I have to make you, because you simply won't lie down of your own accord. But I am making you lie down in a green pasture right now.

Beloved, I am leading you beside quiet waters, waters that you can drink from that will not overwhelm you; the water that I provide for your refreshment. I am restoring your life.

Beloved, I am guiding you in the path of righteousness, the right path. My path for the sake of My great name.

Beloved, even though you are walking through the valley of the shadow of deepest darkness, don't be afraid, for I am with you. I am not standing at the far end of the valley waiting for you to come through, I am with you. We are there together. You and I in the darkness. And while the sides of that valley are so steep, and it is so dark that you cannot see, don't be afraid I am here. I am with you.

My rod is in my hand to protect you. My staff is with Me to tap out the way in the darkness so that you will not be lost. Don't be afraid, My rod and my staff are in my hand to bring you encouragement, to comfort you, to reassure you. I am there. I will never leave you or forsake you.

Beloved, I prepare a table before you even though your enemies are all around. The presence of your enemies cannot prevent Me from preparing a table before you. A table to satisfy you with all good things.

I am anointing your head with oil. Your head, the place where there is so often so much hurt, that I pour My oil upon you, to take the soreness away. The oil upon you now O Beloved, your cup is overflowing.

I tell you this, My dear one, there is absolutely no doubt, no question, that My goodness and My loving kindness will cling to you all the days of your life, and even if your life should end, know this, you and I will dwell together forever and forever.

For I am your Shepherd. I am your Lord. I am your King. I am your God. Be of good cheer. I have overcome the world. Be not afraid, for I am with you. [27]

Both these responses were encouraging and helped me to draw closer to God once again.

It is always easy to look back and to realise that I could never have achieved what I did by 'rushing' ahead of God. In order for anything to be successful you have to find where God is already at work and for the right people to be in place to help you – the right time and the right place!

---

[27] Ministered by the Lord to Chris Hill during a Lydia Conference held in 1991.

CHAPTER 17

Finally To Namibia

God's work, done in God's way, will never lack God's supplies. [28]

Gradually my health improved and the following May I was given the go ahead to book my flight back to Namibia in July. I now had to 'step out of the boat' and sink or swim, as I had no idea what lay ahead.

But once again nothing was straightforward and for another year I would still be searching to find exactly why God had brought me to Namibia. However it was good to be back with friends again and to have all my own things around me. In fact it was difficult to believe I had been away for nearly a year. The cockerel was still crowing all through the night, the water supply was off and on, as was the phone, which ran off a solar panel, and of course all the different insects that had their seasons of visiting. One of the worst were the stink bugs which, although small and harmless and only 'stunk' when you

---

[28] Hudson Taylor (1832-1905) was a Protestant Christian missionary working in China. He founded the China Inland Mission now OMF International.

trod on them by mistake, did get everywhere including my bed. In fact on several occasions when I travelled home I would find one or two carcasses in my suitcase!

Fortunately malaria was not prevalent in this area, but I still slept under a mossie net. I managed to break several pairs of glasses trying to kill the odd one that got under the net. It is not easy trying to kill them when you are standing on a bed, as inevitably you find yourself lying on the bed on top of your glasses! The worst experience I had was when I had been away for a while and on the second night home felt ants crawling all over me and discovered a nest under my mattress – the heat of my body had helped to hatch the young! Thankfully God continued to give me all the grace I needed to cope with everything.

On the first morning after my arrival I attended a weekly meeting of all the church workers during which we had a bible study with discussion, prayers for one another and talked about any problems that needed to be sorted out. The meetings had been going on for a few weeks now and it was good to feel part of a team supporting one another. They also mainly spoke in English for my benefit which was a great help. Various outreach work was being done including youth work, a soup kitchen, Sunday schools, worship and dance groups, teaching in schools, helping in the old age people's home and a bible school; Dawie had started.

Then, on the following Sunday Boet began an early morning service which was mainly held for the benefit of people whose second language was English. They included Government workers from the north and people from overseas and it was wonderful as it helped me feel so much more at home.

My biggest disappointment though, as I quickly discovered, was that the church was no longer going to Bushmanland to do any ministry. Instead the Bushmen trainee pastors were coming to see Dawie every six weeks for training. However Dawie was still travelling to two different areas in the north for bible teaching, so it was suggested that I went with him to teach basic healthcare to the women. So for the time being I had to be content that this was what God wanted me to do.

So I travelled with Dawie to Ondangwa where he had about eighty students. We camped in the grounds of the local AFM church which was a few miles outside the town in the bush and about five minutes from the main road. During this particular outreach we were joined by a small international team from South Africa who had come to do some teaching on Evangelism, paint a local school and at the end of the week help at a Youth Conference being held at the church. One of the team members, Pam, was from Australia and we immediately got on well together so while Dawie was busy teaching I had some company.

For three afternoons, after the women had finished their classes, I taught on different aspects of healthcare. About thirty attended and we sat under a tree in the shade – not always a good place to be when you are constantly being bombarded by ripe fruit falling to the ground and the women in the front row rushing to pick them up! However they were very receptive and I so enjoyed the teaching and had an excellent interpreter. I talked to them about the most important times to wash their hands – why does the mention of 'bowels' always make people laugh, even the older ones! – and how to make water clean to drink. Finally I showed them a way to make 'a special drink' for when they had diarrhoea or vomiting and to recognise the signs of dehydration. One lady would then demonstrate it back to the others. Each lesson finished with questions and then they sang and danced a song they had made up to remember what they had learnt.

I also sat in on some of the bible students' lessons. The students were so enthusiastic and so hungry to learn about God. We had a church service every morning for the students and another one in the evening for anyone. The first night there were about 300 people and then each following night the numbers kept increasing until, when most of the youth came for the Conference on the Thursday, there must have been 700 – 800 people. By this time the service was held outside as the church was not big enough – a wonderful time of worshipping, dancing and prayer, although not at 2.45am when one group arrived singing as loud as they could!

We also went to Ohangwena, near the Angolan border, where Dawie had a further 40 students. Once again we camped in the grounds of the AFM church, but this time the camping was very basic with no 'mod cons' although Dawie had brought a portable loo with him. It was even hotter here with lots of mosquitoes and I found the teaching harder, mainly because the interpreter did not speak very good English and so it took longer for the women to understand what I was saying. The church did not have its own water supply, so water had to be collected from a nearby home. The next time Dawie went there he was able to take some money donated by Jane and Antonia, a friend of hers, and by me, to have the water supply connected to the church. I then received a lovely letter from the Pastor's wife:

'My beloved Mum, I thank you very much for the job you have done for us by give us water. If you were not there, nothing we could do, because water is too expensive. Without water we cannot live. I thank you very much. As the scriptures

said without the word of God there is no live. This is also same water. Nobody can live without. Therefore I thank you for your good job. Thank you very much. God may bless you, keep it up and may our love continue to love us. May wonderful love of Jesus leads you ever and ever. Ame.'

The water supply had cost £20.

As the year ended I had an opportunity to visit Bushmanland again with a friend, but the doors were still firmly closed. What did God want me to do? Had He given me a heart for the Bushmen in order to bring me to Namibia for another purpose? Did He have something special for me to do? At this present time there were no answers to these questions.

Christmas that year was spent with the Carters in Worcester – a good holiday with lots of fellowship, as well as plenty of rest and relaxation. However the New Year left me feeling even more restless and I once again had mixed feelings about where my future lay. So when I returned to Grootfontein I decided to look on the internet for jobs with other missionary organizations working with Bushmen, and found that The Flying Mission in Botswana had an opening for someone to work with their AIDS ministry and applied for the post. But was I giving up too quickly and shutting the door on what God had brought me to Namibia for?

A few weeks later I heard from The Flying Mission and flew to Gaborone for an interview. It was an interesting visit, but after a few days it was obvious on both sides that it was not the right job or place for me to be.

I was only away for about a week and when I got back several things had changed. First of all a new coffee shop had opened at a local nursery which sold cappuccinos and excellent food as well as plants, so at last there was a good place to go and meet up with friends! With my time on the farm coming to an end this gave me the opportunity to find a flat in town and so be in closer contact with the rest of the church team. And six months later I was able to move again to another flat next door to Linda.

A new school had also been opened in the squatter camp, Blikkiesdorp, and the soup kitchen was now being run from there. The school had no electricity, phone line, tables, chairs and other equipment, but eventually all these would be in place. The children were healthy, probably due to the soup kitchen, but many did not have warm clothing and so when it was cold they did not come to school. In time all the children would be provided with the means to purchase a uniform. As there was a lack of anything for the children to play with or on, a friend in YWAM sent me some money and with the help of the Dominee of the Dutch Reform Church, Dirk, and a group of local volunteers, swings, seesaw, tyres and oil drums were soon in place.

Finally as I drove around town I began to ask myself why I wanted to move somewhere different. I knew where all the shops were, had somewhere to go for a cappuccino, and the opportunity for new ministries were opening up. At long last I was beginning to feel at home!

In my diary I wrote:

'Father, I feel such an excitement and stirring in my spirit. I feel You are 'on the move' and I must be ready to move with You or I will be left behind and not receive all the blessings You have for me and others. 'New beginnings' are about to happen. And it feels wonderful! That was yesterday Father. This morning I wake up and it is cool and cloudy outside and I feel low for some reason. The question of 'using the gifts God has given you' comes to mind and Father I don't

know what gifts You have given me. Please reveal them to me, so I can use them to fulfil Your purpose here on earth. Thank you Father that I can come to You about anything and everything – that I can share my 'ups' and 'downs' with you at any time of the day or night.'

It was now time for me to go home again for a short visit and for the first time since Michael married again and moved to New Zealand, both of us would be in England at the same time. So I sent him an email asking if we could meet again and I also told him how I had forgiven him over the break-up of our marriage and hoped he would forgive me. He replied that he did not want to meet up again as there was no point in bringing up the past – the last thing I wanted to do anyway – and wished me well in my endeavours. I had thought it would be a good opportunity to talk about the girls and to learn what each of us was doing. Anyway it was his choice and all I could do was pray that one day he would accept Jesus into his heart and be able to put the past behind him and move on.

As soon as I returned to Grootfontein I was busy sorting out my new flat, buying furniture and settling down again. I acquired a puppy called Peppy who was about nine weeks old, a cross between a dachshund and fox terrier. She was adorable, had lots of character and was a great companion.

Then finally God revealed to me what all the preparation time in Zimbabwe, Mozambique, South Africa and now Namibia had been for. Winston Churchill once said, 'To each there comes in his or her lifetime a special moment when they are tapped on the shoulder and offered the chance to do a very special thing, unique to them and fitted to their talent. What a tragedy if that moment finds them unprepared or unqualified for that which could have been their finest hour'.

Boet had been attending the annual meeting of all the AFM pastors during which time a representative from Catholic Aids Action (CAA), Lucy Steinitz, had been encouraging the church to become involved in the AIDs pandemic. CAA ran a 'Training of Trainers' (TOT) course in Windhoek where you could learn how to train volunteers in home-based care, counselling and working with orphans. Boet had offered to start a project in the Grootfontein area, which the AFM church would support for the first year and had been asked to choose one or two people to attend the course. When Boet told me about this I had a 'Holy Spirit' moment when I knew without doubt that this was what God wanted me to do – I had indeed been 'tapped on the shoulder'.

So within a few weeks I found myself attending the course which lasted for eight months, divided into four phases, of which five weeks were in the classroom in Windhoek and in between assignments had to be completed, along with a personal journal of our field work.

There were about twenty students, 13 women and 7 men, some of whom worked for CAA and others were nurses, counsellors, NGOs or had been sent by their churches. I was the only white person and as usual the oldest! I learnt a great deal during this time especially from the other students relating to their culture, their everyday problems and the large differences between rural and urban communities. We were also given an excellent teaching aid called John's Story which explained, with pictures, how easy it was to become infected with HIV.

My first assignment was to hold an 'AIDS Awareness Day'.

CHAPTER 18

HIV/AIDS Project Begins

"Lord, let me make a difference for you that is utterly disproportionate to who I am"[29]

God then began to move quickly and I was hard pressed to keep up with Him! Dominee Dirk offered to take me around town to see what was happening regarding HIV/AIDS work and who was doing what. The hospital and the local clinic in the location were doing some counselling and treatment. The local Red Cross was going to begin some training of home-based care workers and the Municipality was in the process of setting up some 'in-house' training.

We obtained some statistics and out of a population of 21,000 people there were 500 illegal outlets for the sale of beer and alcohol, and seventeen streets where prostitutes could be found. With a large Army base situated on the edge of town and Grootfontein being on a main transport corridor route, they all helped to contribute to the spread of HIV. The most prevalent medical conditions we learnt were STDs, malaria,

---

[29] John Piper. From a sermon titled, 'Making a difference by Fire'. October 2nd 1989. See End Notes.

TB and HIV/AIDS, with diarrhoea and headaches at the end of the list. The town also had the second highest rate of infection for mother-to-child transmission with 29% of pregnant women infected and the town was now known as 'Aidsfontein'. At this time it was estimated that 22% of the population of Namibia – 1.8 million – were infected and it was already impacting society with more than over 100,000 orphans living in extended families.

There was a local Action Aids Committee, but with only three members left little action had taken place for some time. So after speaking with the present Chairman, I was able, with his help, to set up a new Grootfontein Aids Committee consisting of key community members and health workers, including the Hospital Superintendent who was to be a great support in all that we set out to achieve. The idea was that they would meet on a regular basis so that there was no duplication of the work being done and to use each other's expertise and skills. All were very supportive that the AFM church wanted to be involved.

I reported my findings back to Boet, and along with Pastor Bertie, Pastor of the 'Body of Christ' church, the AFM church situated in the location, Omulunga, we met to discuss how we could set up an Awareness Session on HIV/AIDS which would comply with my first assignment for the TOT course. We then decided to go beyond this and set up a centre in the church, to be known as The Hope Centre, where people could obtain any information they needed concerning HIV/AIDS. We then planned to extend these Hope Centres, along with training in HIV/AIDS Awareness, to other communities where the AFM had churches.

To launch the project Pastor Bertie arranged a special service dedicated to HIV awareness and I met up with church members who were interested in taking part. We decided to perform a drama based on John's Story and I was asked if the drama could have more of a Christian feel to it which also included bringing in a witch doctor to the story! I was delighted with this as it meant the drama would be coming from them and not be my idea. A choir was formed to sing some songs and I suggested buying some candles to be lit in memory of those who had died from AIDS and hope for those who were HIV+. We also decided to make red ribbon bows, the symbol for HIV/AIDS, for everyone to wear. Finally I would give a short message.

I was very moved when I walked into the church, a large tent, on the day of the service. Everywhere was decorated in red and white and as people entered the church they were given an 'AIDS' ribbon to wear. There were about 60 people present. The service went well and I was able to speak on the basic facts about HIV/AIDS, information about the town regarding alcohol and prostitution and God's role in all of this. I ended with a request that all those people who were interested in being involved in the Hope Centre should come the following evening for a meeting. We ended the service with people lighting one hundred candles and many tears were shed.

The following evening about thirty people turned up for the meeting and during discussions I discovered that a number of people had already been trained in home-based care and counselling but had not known what to do next – God had been preparing the ground! Everyone was very keen that the church should become a training base for volunteers to go and help those who were sick at home, counsel those infected with HIV and learn how to care for orphans and other vulnerable children.

So it was agreed that immediately after the official opening of the Hope Centre the following February, I would run a day course on HIV/AIDS and AIDS Awareness. The following week we would start our first two-week course on Home-based Care, along with courses on Counselling and Psycho-Support for Orphans and Other Vulnerable Children. Then when Pastor Bertie's house was finished being built, next to the church, we would have an office there.

For some reason I had never imagined that I would be so quickly involved in setting up a project, which in time would require funding from overseas, and teaching about AIDS and Home-based Care. I really did not feel confident in doing any of this at all, but if it was what God had been preparing me for, then I knew He would give me all the guidance, skills and help I needed – I was also discovering where my gifts lay!

My main work was to be with Bertie's church where the congregation was mainly Damara, along with Herero, Kavango, Ovamboland and Bushmen all living in the location and at Blikkiesdorp. There was a great need for locally run initiatives and training so that people could go into their own communities and give 'grass-roots' education, almost on a one-to-one basis. We would also train people in Otavi the next town to Grootfontein and cover three Bushmen communities, one in Omotako, in Bushmanland and the other two in Bravo and Tsintsabis, both Haikom Bushmen communities not far from Etosha, National Park. In several of the Bushmen communities we had discovered that the older women were now going to the shabeens (alcohol outlets) for sex with younger men (mostly from other tribal groups) in order to earn some money and there had been a few confirmed cases of HIV.

At long last I was able to work with the Bushman. God was now revealing the 'bigger' picture in which my work was to extend across all the tribal groups of Namibia, not just the Bushman. John Wesley once said 'Do all you can, by all the means you can, in all the ways you can, in all the places you can, at all the times you can, to all the people you can, as long as ever you can' and this was what I was hoping to do with God's help.

December was a very quiet month for me as everyone was away on holiday, and it gave me a chance to spend time preparing and planning for the following year. This included Aids Awareness and Home-based Care teaching notes, designing various forms for record keeping and monitoring, and guidelines so that as we opened more Hope Centres they would be run more or less in the same way. I also prepared certificates to give to the students when they had completed their courses and got together Home-based Care Kits for each volunteer.

Finally I designed a T-shirt which had the project's logo on the front and on the back the words 'Cure Aids God's Way' and underneath '1 Thes.4: 1-8'.[30] I was beginning to appreciate how much work went into running courses – it was much easier being a student! Fortunately I did have a lot of support

---

[30] Finally, brothers, we instructed you how to live in order to please God, as in fact you are living. Now we ask you and urge you in the Lord Jesus to do this more and more. For you know what instructions we gave you by the authority of the Lord Jesus. It is God's will that you should be sanctified: that you should avoid sexual immorality; that each of you should learn to control his own body in a way that is holy and honourable, not in passionate lust like the heathen who do not know God; and that in this matter no one should wrong his brother to take advantage of him. The Lord will punish men for all such sins, as we have already told you and warned you. For God did not call us to be impure, but to live a holy life. Therefore, he who rejects this instruction does not reject man but God, who give you his Holy Spirit.

and help during this time from both the Hospital and the Red Cross.

At the beginning of January a couple from South Africa, Andre and Anita, came to stay to see if their church could regularly send teams to help with the different aspects of the church's work. They planned to start in two Bushmen communities in early April which would include me teaching on Aids Awareness. Anita spent some time helping me to improve my teaching notes so they became more interesting and lively by having more student participation and this was a tremendous help.

One day we went to visit Dawie and Trudie and during a time of prayer, Anita saw a picture of me walking in the bush pushing aside "landmines" that others behind me would deal with. I would go in front to begin preparing the way so others could come behind to complete the work. I would receive a very similar prophecy a few months later in which God said He would bring people in from all over to carry on the work.

There then followed a few busy and difficult weeks trying to work out a budget for running the courses with no real idea of how much things would cost. This included providing food, buying T-shirts and home-based care kits and travel costs, all of which would be acceptable to the AFM Executive Committee. At the same time it was the rainy season with temperatures reaching 40C, so there were moments when I felt I was sinking into quicksand – what would happen if it all cost too much and the whole idea of having a training centre fell apart? Thankfully I knew God was with me and guiding me and 'all will be well'. He also gave me a great deal of grace as there were times when I became very frustrated and irritated, but knowing at the same time if I was doing this back home the same problems would probably arise!

A few weeks before the courses began I received approval from the Executive Committee to go ahead with all my proposals and budgets – which was just as well as it was too late to stop the work now!

February soon came round and our official opening of the first Hope Centre by the Mayor of Grootfontein, along with several key people. The day started with a service and then we ran our Aids Awareness Course, which included talking about HIV/AIDS, using John's Story, playing games, and finally a True or False quiz. In all about twenty-five people attended including some people from a couple of AFM churches in nearby communities. It was a great success with many misconceptions about HIV/AIDS being sorted out and everyone went away with a Certificate in Aids Awareness. They were now equipped to go into their communities to give the correct information and advice concerning all aspects of HIV and AIDS.

On the following Monday the courses began with nine ladies attending the Home-based Care course and one lady, Selena, who was HIV+, came when she was well enough. Two of the ladies were illiterate and one of these two was breast feeding her eighth child! They were a wonderful group, so hard working and fun to be with. I had asked several experts from the hospital and Red Cross to come and give some of the lectures. Then during the second week they spent time on the wards at the local hospital being assessed by the nursing staff on various skills. On the final Friday I set them a test on what they had learnt. They all passed with flying colours and were very appreciative about the course having enjoyed it very much. From the nine I was able to choose two, Ponde and Elizabeth, who would be able to teach on subsequent courses. Sadly Selena died shortly afterwards.

By the time all the courses had finished we had trained about sixty people in the different disciplines. Now it was time to reach out to those in need, both physically and spiritually, and to start removing the misconceptions and stigmatism that surround HIV and AIDS. At a service soon afterwards the students received their certificates and home-based care kits – an inspiring time of celebration, and a sense of having achieved something worthwhile.

Shortly after the courses finished I received some wonderful news from Louise. She rang me up to say that she and Roger (her partner of eight years) were going to get married in August. Roger had proposed to her on Sheepstor, one of our favourite places on Dartmoor. She then emailed a photo they had taken of themselves on the Tor, both looking so happy. So I was now going to be planning an unexpected trip home in August.

In early April I went with Dawie and Trudie for an outreach to Tsintsabis where we were joined by a team from Andre and Anita's church and it turned out to be one of the best outreaches I had been on and a very memorable one.

Amongst the team of twelve were Estelle, who was a nurse, and a couple called Pieter and Maven. Estelle and I did some HIV/AIDS teaching and this time it was very different as most of the Bushmen knew nothing about the virus, so we had to make it very simple. Estelle was happy to demonstrate the use of condoms to the ladies, but not when we spoke to the men, so one of the men offered to do the demonstration, using the handle of a rake to put the condom on. Estelle told him to gently blow the end before putting it on, but he blew it rather hard and it came up like a balloon, which made everyone laugh!

One day we went to Bravo, another Bushmen community, and this time we had to make the teaching even more simple, as it was spoken through three interpreters, so we told them about life choices, whether they wanted to choose when they died or when God had planned.

One morning during team devotions I had had an enormous breakthrough in my relationship with God and how He saw me. During my own personal time of prayer I was reading one of Joni Eareckson Tada's devotional books in which she wrote about how 'At the moment of the most-free choice, it feels most like a destiny, and at the moment when you feel destined to make a certain choice, it feels so free... C. S. Lewis's explanation of this principle is: 'When you obey God in wholehearted devotion, you step closer toward his idea of who he has determined you to be: the real you, the you he predetermined before the foundation of the world. This means that when you obey God, in the process you discover who you are. You know yourself better than before. You become the more excellent you, and therefore you step into your destiny. What freedom! And it can happen to you today as you obey.'[31]

These words of C.S. Lewis really spoke to me, so I decided to share them with the team – and I am so glad I did! Having explained that I had experienced three fathers before I was five years old, Pieter was led to pray that God would become 'My Father'. This was then followed by Dawie and Maven praying and having words for me.

Estelle then danced a prophecy. She had never been led to do this before and I had never experienced receiving one. It was beautiful and as she danced around the tented church she

---

[31] Joni Eareckson Tasa, *More Precious Than Silver*, Zondervan, 1998. 11 April.

told me how God had watched over me all my life and that He loved me. He had seen what the devil had stolen, but now He would restore 'all that the locusts have eaten'.[32]

I was then finally able to forgive all the people who had hurt me over the years – the past was gone and I was now ready to start a new life. God also revealed Himself to me – it was like the Cross, when I gave my life to Jesus – but this time it was God in all His glory. God was finally and completely out of His 'box'!

I then knew that it was time for me to have a full-emersion baptism so that all my sins and past could be washed away and I would become a new person. As Dawie was going to baptise six Bushmen that evening in a pool which had been dug out of the sand, I decided to join them. It was the right time and the right place and a wonderful experience – I had discovered who I am.

---

[32] Joel 2: 25a.

CHAPTER 19

Finding the Funding

*Let us not become weary in doing good for at the proper
time we will reap a harvest if we do not give up.*

(Gal. 6:9)

Following a trip to South Africa to visit friends, I went back to
Ondangwa with Dawie and Trudie so I could see about setting
up a Hope Centre there. It was a good visit in spite of the
thousands of flies and being so cold at night I had to go and
buy a hot water bottle! I had not realised that the students who
attended Dawie's bible school came from nearly thirty
different congregations and they all wanted to do something to
help with the HIV crisis. Again the task of helping the people
seemed very daunting. But something had to be done because
in the rural areas there were few if any medical facilities, and
with a total lack of knowledge about HIV/AIDS, the AFM
churches would have an opportunity to help their people once
they were trained. I was reminded of a Breton fisherman's
prayer: 'Lord, the sea is so large and my boat is so small'.

With the AFM church soon to stop funding the project,
money had to be found from other sources and more people

needed to be brought in to help with the administrative side of organising the training and setting up of the Hope Centres. Where did I begin? So I turned to God and He gave me His promise: 'Since you are precious and honoured in my sight, and because I love you, I will give men in exchange for you, and people in exchange for your life'.[33] – I was not alone. And in fact as I sat at my laptop in the months to come preparing proposals for funding from major overseas donors I would have no idea what to write or where to start, so I would pray and God would show me what needed to be written and slowly the funding came in.

We had a donation from Bank Windhoek, from a local mill to supply mealie meal for the soup kitchen and blankets from The Lions Club, which we distributed to those who were sick. One lady said she could now sleep at night and another man who was dying was very grateful for the extra warmth as the winter time temperatures were dropping to 3C. Boet then learnt about a small grant being given by UNAIDS which we could apply for in order to run some more courses the following year. This involved a lot more than just writing a 'begging' letter. I needed to decide how many volunteers we could train, then get quotations for every single item we needed, which once again included food for the students, travel costs, T-shirts and home-based care kits. Every cent had to be accounted for.

Although at times I would find myself getting bogged down with all that had to be done and the problems that often arose, I had plenty of support and encouragement from Boet, Dawie and Linda. And I would also be encouraged at the hard work Bertie and all his volunteers were doing on their own initiative.

---

[33] Isaiah 43:4.

Help then came in a sudden and unexpected way. Lucy Steinitz had kept in contact since we began the Hope Centres and was now working for Family Health International as their Senior Technical Officer for Faith Based Programmes. They were the agents for USAID, an initiative from George Bush to give emergency funding to countries in need. Following an email I had written to USAID asking how we applied for funding to keep the project going, Lucy contacted Boet to see if she could come for a visit. A report had to be written on what we had been doing, what our future plans were and of course a budget, but it was all worthwhile.

I drove to Tsumeb Airport to collect Lucy and took her straight to see the soup kitchen where over 800 children – many being orphans – were now being fed daily during term time. We then went to see Bertie and some of the volunteers at work. We visited a lady who was Mary's age, 32 years, but looked in her sixties. She was very sick with Aids but was being well looked after by the volunteers. Sadly she died a few days later and left four children, with the oldest at fifteen to bring up the rest of the family.

By this time over forty people had visited the Centre for general advice, thirty-eight were undergoing counselling, seventeen people being nursed in their homes – four of whom died – and thirty-four orphans identified. It was a very successful visit, but if funding was given it would change a great many things, one of which was that we would become an NGO (Non-Government Organisation). It would also entail attending regular meetings in Windhoek, a five hour journey, and we would need someone to look after the accounts. Money would also be available to pay Bertie and someone to take over my job. Suddenly the project was growing again. However we first had to make our application for funding for the year 2005-2006, which I did with Lucy and Boet's help.

Before I flew back home for Louise's wedding I spent a day in Omatako teaching on Aids Awareness to about fifty Bushmen from the AFM congregation. It was so cold we had to do a lot of singing and dancing to keep warm! SPAR, the local super market, had donated boxes of apples and oranges so with Boet, who came with me, we handed them out to three different Bushmen communities. The smiles of joy on all their faces were wonderful.

The day of Louise and Roger's wedding turned out to be one of the very few dry days of August we had that summer. Louise looked stunning in her dress and Mary, Jane and a niece of Roger's, Fran, were her bridesmaids and also looked beautiful. Much to Louise's surprise Roger had organised a 1919 car to take her to the church which all added to the occasion. It was lovely seeing so many friends and family there. The service went well and I read one of the readings. Roger looked very proud having at last made the right decision to marry Louise and both of them spoke up clearly when making their vows. Several people remarked afterwards that they had not been to a church wedding for a long time and enjoyed it very much.

For the first few days back in Grootfontein I struggled to readjust and felt homesick especially when I was looking at all the photographs of Louise's wedding. I did miss being involved in the girl's day to day lives. Once again I was wondering where my life was going and what I was going to happen next with the project.

But I did not have to wait long before God was on the move again. Firstly I received news that we had been successful in our bid for funding from UNAIDS to train more volunteers the following year. It seemed that our project had been impressive and because we and the Red Cross were the only two organisations working in the Grotfontein area on combating HIV/AIDS, we were given the grant. We would now be able to train fifty more volunteers in a combined course of home-based care, counselling and working with orphans, which meant that in rural areas there would be more volunteers who were equipped to help in all the disciplines. A number of these volunteers would be trained in the north by six people who were at present being trained by CAA in the TOT course.

A short time later Lucy came to visit again to discuss with Boet and myself how to expand our work, apply for funding and set up a solid structure, especially concerning manpower. Within a matter of a few weeks Boet was appointed the National Co-ordinator of AFM Aids Action, as it was now going to be called, and I became Project Manager and Co-ordinator of Training and Programmes. Our aims were to assist communities by providing volunteers trained in home-based care, counselling and working with orphans and other vulnerable children; following tried and tested methods of teaching AIDS prevention, including workshops and simple drama; making available to the community help and advice on all aspects of HIV and AIDS; actively encouraging Positive Living and addressing the stigma associated with HIV and AIDS.

In October Grootfontein began to administer anti-retroviral (ARV) drugs and medication for infected pregnant mothers and their babies – only one of eight hospitals in Namibia at that time. So our volunteers, when more Government funding became available, would be trained to help patients take the ARVs on a regular basis and also help in the administration of TB treatment.

We then received a grant from the Church Alliance for Orphans to set up an 'after-school' club at the church, to be known as The Hope Club, for thirty-five orphans to begin with. This was run by Emerencia and Maria. The idea was for the children to meet twice a week in the afternoons for games, various activities and Bible stories. They would also be washed and clothed if necessary and given some food. Counselling would be on hand for those who needed it. By doing this we felt the children could support one another and have somewhere they could come for love and hugs. By March of the following year the club had grown to seventy-five children, although they did not all turn up at the same time. We also received funding from a Catholic Church in Germany which paid for showers and toilets to be built for the children and anyone else's use.

Applying for funding from overseas donors took a long time as so much data was required. At this time I was not only applying for money from USAIDS, but also from another donor Geneva Global, who gave funding to 'faith-based grass-roots' organisations but had never given one to a Pentecostal church before, so that became quite a challenge. When I thought I had completed the form, it would be returned for more details or our ideas would have to change. During this time Boet taught me never to limit God and to ask for more than we felt we needed at this time. God would provide exactly what we needed.

Geneva Global also required testimonies from people receiving home-based care and those attending The Hope Club. These I obtained with the help of Bertie and it was good to get some feedback:

'M was visited by the Home-based Care volunteers on three different occasions. She told them that she was treated with great respect and they prayed with her. After their first visit she felt like a human being again. The volunteers are also making her more aware of God and encouraging her in the word of God. M wants the Hope Centre and the volunteers to continue doing their work as she feels they make people who are sick more comfortable with their sickness. M is so happy that she has become a Christian after the volunteers encouraged her to come to Christ'.

'J was visited by the Home-base Care volunteers twice in one month. She was treated very well and they prayed with her on every occasion and gave her the word of God. She felt very good about the volunteers work on behalf of the sick people and it made her also more aware about the work of God and about Christ in one's personal life. J says the volunteers are doing a good job, because it made her more aware that when family members take care of their own sick they are often quite negligent. J wants the Hope Centre volunteers to continue their good work in Christ as they are always there for her in her time of need and for prayer. The volunteers are also always open with her and she feels more secure being taken care by them'.

'G is 12 years old and attends 'The Hope Club'. He loves coming to the club because he receives love and care. Having support has helped him a lot as he feels like he was with his own parents and it makes him feel good. G has learnt to make friends with the other children, to play games with them, to learn how to pray and all this makes him feel good. The food he is given is also good. He would like to have books to read, especially a bible, playground equipment and toys. When he sees the volunteers they make him feel so happy and comfortable'.

(G lives with his grandmother. His father died in Zimbabwe some years ago and his mother died in 2000).

'S is 8 years old and finds the support she is given by 'The Hope Club' makes her feel very good. She is meeting and making more friends and feels free to talk to the volunteers because they give her support and good care. She wants the volunteers to continue to give her good care and support as long as she needs it'.

(M lives with her mother who is too old to take proper care of her. She has a 4 year old sister who also comes to 'The Hope Club' and she is very small for her age and malnourished).

CHAPTER 20

Homeward Bound

But God chose the foolish things of the world to shame the wise; God chose the weak things of the world to shame the strong.

(I Cor 1:27)

It was now coming to the time of the year again when most people went away for their long summer holidays and so I found myself mainly on my own once more. Suddenly all my desires to be in Namibia began to fade away – I did not want to be here anymore. Jane was having a great deal of pain again in her hip and was going to see David Hunt about a replacement. I should be at home to support her and not thousands of miles away. It was also an exceptionally hot and rainy season, and I continually felt tired trying to cope with temperatures in the 40s, not always feeling very well, wanting to live in my own culture and to be near my children.

But at the same time I wanted to be in God's will and be obedient to Him. So life seemed to be a constant struggle, and I had no peace. I was constantly praying that God would help me to be patient and to trust that, when the time was right, He would release me to go home. But what would I do when I finally got home? What did the future hold?

As I had been home for Louise's wedding, Christmas was spent quietly in Grootfontein again. My 60th birthday in the New Year was very different to what I had planned, expecting to be back in England, but it was enjoyable nevertheless. Linda and I went to Tsumeb for lunch and wandered around the shops. Then in the evening, Jurgen and Anna, our neighbours organised a braai (BBQ) for me. I was also able to talk to the girls on the phone and other friends around the world and enjoyed opening my cards and presents.

As the year progressed more volunteers were trained, giving us a total of fifty-eight people working from eight Hope Centres, five in the Grootfontein area and three in the north. Frequent outreaches were also taking place, mostly in the rural areas, teaching on Aids Awareness. Many sick people were being reached, and counselled, and orphans taken care of. Our proposal was accepted by USAID and we would receive funding from that April. This meant we were able to give salaries to key workers and much to my relief a friend of Boet's, Doreen, became our accountant. Boet remained the National Co-ordinator, Bertie the Regional Field Leader, Johannes took over my job as Co-ordinator for Training and Programmes and I became the Overseas Volunteer. Linda was appointed Co-ordinator for Relief and Development. The National and Regional Offices, as they became, were moved from my flat into two of the rooms in Bertie's home and new office equipment purchased. Everything was coming together now and I would soon be able to hand over my work to the Namibians.

And so I began to feel that my time in Namibia was really coming to an end now and God was calling me home.

During a church service Magda had sung a prophecy in which she said, 'Sometimes you feel anxious, angry, or sorry for yourself; in your marriage, relationships or place that you are in. But even this is part of My plan. I know what you need. In order to hear Me your emotions must be quiet. I operate in an atmosphere of obedience, joy and faith. I know what you need, better than you know yourself.'

Those words really spoke to me, as I was still finding it difficult to quieten my emotions, so that I could hear God clearly about the future. I also knew that every time I spoke doubt over my future I was sewing negative seeds, shaping my outlook, creating a self-fulfilling prophecy and most of all contradicting the God who said 'The plans I have for you are good'.[34]

However, events were taking place back in England which meant that I would have to make a short trip home before, I finally left Namibia. Some months before Jane had injured her left knee while dancing and it had turned out more serious than first thought with her kneecap being completely displaced. Eventually after an MRI scan the decision was made to operate and this took place at the end of May. As Jane felt she could cope without me being there I remained in Grootfontein. Mary was there for her during the day of the operation, before she flew out to New Zealand to stay with her father. Louise then went to stay with Jane for a few days when she came out of hospital. However Jane soon realised that she needed someone to help her as recovery was going to take longer than she had thought. So within a matter of days I found myself flying back to England to take care of her for a month.

---

[34] Bob and Debby Gass with Ruth Gass Haliday, *The UCB Word for Today*. Day 31.10.02. See End Notes.

When I was back in Namibia I was once again drafting a new budget for 2006/7 for USAID, which was not easy as it was difficult to know what would be happening in two years' time, but as the budget would be increased by 2.5 times more than the present year it was also challenging and exciting.

At the same time my work permit was coming to an end and although I had submitted a renewal I had not heard whether it had been successful or not. For some reason about ten days before my present permit expired I decided to go to the local Home Affairs office to see what would happen if I remained in the country after that date. I was told that I would not be able to leave the country until my work permit application had been processed which could be several months.

It was time to leave – the waiting was over and God was releasing me from my work. It was just as He had spoken through a prophecy the previous year, I 'had begun the work for others to take over' and 'my work would come to a sudden close'. I now had to 'Trust in the Lord with all *my* heart and lean not on *my* own understanding; in all *my* ways acknowledge him, and he will make *my* paths straight'[35] for the future.

So within a few days I had finished my packing, sold the things I was not taking with me and said 'goodbye' to all my friends and left Peppy with Linda. Although it was a sudden and tearful farewell, I had total peace that it was the right time to go and on the 14th August I arrived back in England to begin a new season in my life.

I left knowing I had achieved something that not many have the opportunity to do. And I felt humbled by this. God had led me to begin this project in a small town in the north of

---

[35] Proverbs 3: 5-6.

Namibia, where so little was being done to help those infected and affected with HIV and AIDS. I had gone to bear fruit and now I knew that the fruit would last. God was still there helping the others to continue with the work for as long as it was needed.

An African Proverb says: 'If you think you are too small to make a difference try sleeping in a closed room with a mosquito'. I have done that and been blessed in so many ways by God, not least with my three wonderful girls, finding my birth parents and making many friends around the world. Most of all though I have found my true identity and a very special Father, who would always and forever love me for who I am – His precious daughter, Wendy.

EPILOGUE

The spiritual life is the life of a child. We are not uncertain of God, just uncertain of what He is going to do next... But when we have the right relationship with God, life is full of spontaneous, joyful uncertainty and expectancy... Leave everything to Him and it will be gloriously and graciously uncertain how He will come in – but you can be certain that He will come. Remain faithful to Him.[36]

Since I gave my life to Jesus it has been very much a time of restoration, healing of past hurt and understanding the meaning of forgiveness and being forgiven. But most of all, discovering my true identity and how precious I am to Him.

My work for the Kingdom has played a very tiny part in it all – my relationship with Jesus has been the most important, knowing that I could never live any other way.

And the future I was worried about? Louise and Roger presented me with twin granddaughters, Grace and Rose, bringing with them their own unique love.

---

[36] Oswald Chambers, *My Utmost of His Highest*, Christian Art Publishers, 1993. April 29.

Mary is now living in Canada with her Canadian boyfriend and is very happy, and they are shortly to be married.

Jane has had both of her hips successfully replaced, surgery to stabilise her stomach and recently open heart surgery to replace part of her aortic route. God has been healing Jane – not in the way I had imagined, by some miracle, but by the skills of her surgeons and modern medicine.

Mum still lives in Neepawa, Canada, and we speak to each other regularly.

The AFMAA project continues and with funding from Geneva Global the work has expanded into Bushmanland with over fifty home-based care volunteers being trained to cover a number of different communities.

What next? I have no idea. It is very much in God's hands. I still have my 'dreams, vision and goals' and pray that one day they will be fulfilled. I discovered 'my beach dream' a little while ago on an island off the south west coast of England. A beautiful beach bathed in bright warm autumn sunlight – only God could have '*turned* my darkness into light'.[37]

I hope that you will find my story is as Joseph Pulitzer said when giving advice to writers: 'Put it before them briefly so they will read it, clearly so they will appreciate it, picturesquely so they will remember it and, above all, accurately so they will be guided by its light'.[38]

---

[37] Psalm 18: 28b.

[38] Joseph Pulitzer (1847-1911) was born in Hungary and became a well-known journalist in the USA.

Aged 5 weeks.

Aged 5 months.

Aged 13 months.

Pictures of me that Mum left with the adoption agency for me
to see if I asked about the adoption.

Aged 2 ½ years.

Aged 3 years.

Aged 4 ½ years: photo taken to show potential adopters.

Aged 5 years: photo taken and sent by adoption agency to
Mum to show her I was happy.

With my new parents the following summer aged 5 years.

With Aunty Mary while on holiday in Cheshire when I visited
the fortune teller, summer 1961.

With my three daughters, Christmas 1976.

Mum and I reunited in Winnipeg, Canada, 1990.

Tina, me and Chris together after 42years, 1991.

Chris, me, Jenny and Ken at Trafalgar Square,
London, 2001.

Font at the church of St Peter and St Paul, Uplyme, Dorset where I was christened, 1992.

Embracing life in Chad, 1998.

In reception doing my work duty: YWAM base The King's Lodge, Nuneaton, 1999.

Feeding the boys a snack: Maforga, Mozambique, 2000.

Fetching water from the well at YWAM base, Dondo,
2000.

Preaching at Aids Awareness Sunday at the Body of
Christ Church, Omulunga, 2002.

With the students after they had completed home-based care, counselling and working with orphans courses, 2003.

Teaching Aids Awareness to the Bushmen at Tsintsabis, 2003.

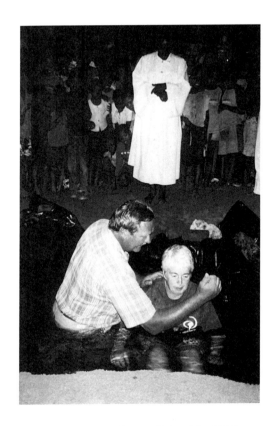

My baptism at Tsintabis, 2003

My 60th birthday: lunch with Linda, in Tsumeb, 2005.

My farewell 'braai' with the team: Marita, Magda, Boet,
Trudie, Sussie, Linda, Dawie, 2005.

End Notes

Footnote 3: Quoted by kind permission of Coventry Cathedral from a welcome guide leaflet arranged by The Revd. Everard Perrens.

Footnote 28: Ministered by The Lord. Also found as an extract from Christopher Hill's booklet 'The Song of the Shepherd'. Copies may be obtained from C L Ministries, 28 Thorney Road, Capel St. Mary, Ipswich IP9 2LH for £2.00 plus postage.

Footnote 30: Piper wrote this prayer in response to the writings of David Brainerd, a missionary to the New England Indians over 200 years ago. Piper continues ....'The prayer contains a disclaimer "I am not great. But you, Lord, are very great. And in your astonishing sovereignty you can let my little life make a difference far beyond all my little powers." Copyright Desiring God. Website: desiringGod.org.

Footnote 35: Free issues of the daily devotional are available for the UK and Republic of Ireland from UCB Operations Centre, Westport Road, Stoke-on-Trent, ST6 4JF. Tel: 0845 60 40 401. Email: ucb@ucb.co.uk

Useful Addresses
(in alphabetical order)

Lee Abbey Christian Community

(Part of the Lee Abbey Movement):

Lynton,

North Devon,

EX35 6JJ.

Tel: 0800 389 1189 or 01598 752 621

Macmillan Cancer Support

89 Albert Embankment

London

SW1 7UQ

Tel: 0207 840 7849

Marfan Association UK

Rochester House

5 Aldershot Road

Fleet

Hampshire

GU51 3NG

Tel: 01252 810 472 or 01252 617 320

Email: contactus@marfan-association.org,uk

SIM

Wetheringsett Manor

Wetheringsett

Stowmarket

Sufolk

IP14 5QX

Tel: 01449 766 464

Email: info@sim.co.uk

WEC International

Bulstrode

Oxford Road

Gerrards Cross

Buckinghamshire

SL9 8SZ

Tel: 0113 282 2291 EXT. 333

Youth With A Mission

6 Highfield Oval

Harpenden

Hertforshire

AL5 $BX

Tel: 01582 463 300

www.ywamharpenden.org